Lucifer's Replacement

By

Kamia White

Studio KWest Publishing Group
Kamia White Kingdom Solutions

Studio KWest Publishing Group
A Division of Kamia White Kingdom Solutions, LLC
Printed in the United States of America
ISBN: 979-8-9859512-1-9 (paperback)

Dedication

This book's dedication is to my parents, the late Mr. and Mrs. Clinton White. Without their sacrifices, my life would not have evolved. My parents taught me valuable lessons that will be with me forever. Their unconditional love for me during my failures gave me the strength to overcome suicide. They helped me rewrite my story and celebrate victories in life.

My great grandmother, Josephine Ridley Butler, departed her life before my birth. Hearing stories about her leadership and prayer life in her community revealed the call upon my life. Many souls came to Christ on her porch as she conducted prayer services. She was very influential in helping establish the First Born Church of the Living God, Inc. It is an honor to continue her legacy.

To the memory of every person part of the LGBTQ community, overwhelmed with rejection and unfair judgments at times, their mental health collapsed. The end resort prompted them to commit suicide to stop the pain of living.

Table of Contents

Foreword

This literary work is genius. Bishop White is an emerging voice of and unto the voiceless that seemingly trapped in the visceral throws of life's choices. This book captures every emotion one can experience. I was captivated by the candor of this work, as the real-life scenarios made it easy to digest. Bishop masterfully divulges the conundrum of humankind after his fall in the Garden of Eden.

The psalmist declares in Psalm 82:5, "...all the foundations of the earth are out of course." Post Eden, everyone born after that was born with a need that only one could fulfill. Therefore, it is truthfully implied that everyone born after the fall of man was born wrongly. Jesus instructs Nicodemus in John 3 that the only way this course correction can occur is through the water and the spirit. One must be born again. The fall of man ushered in so many maladies, and of course, our adversary would exploit humankind to accuse him before the Judge of all the Earth. Man's challenges stem from direct disobedience to God's command— "Do NOT eat...." This exploitation shapes our appetites, and of course, his curse is to feed off the dust(flesh). The content of this literary work entails how one can become ensnared if one's desires are not yielded to the Word of God and His Spirit. Although the author shares her downfalls, the glory of this work is the unwavering patience of God the Father towards those who fall from His grace. As we examine our lives, we note that the Bible is a family story that repeats the lessons of fallen sons. The Father never fails on His part, but the reality of life is we have and will fail as children. The Father is consistent and willing to restore us, but one must acknowledge the wrong and ARISE and return to Him! Bishop Kamia White does just that; she shows how we can lose loved ones in life, and the enemy takes advantage of our broken hearts to create "ENTANGLEMENTS" designed to trap our souls. Amidst the shame, alienation, rebellion, pride, uncleanness, and other countless emotions, we have a God who is committed to our BECOMING. She captures the truth of God not being threatened because we had a mishap.

She manages to remind us of His everlasting love towards us when He could have easily chosen to condemn us to judgment and shame. I simply suggest that you get a nice cup of hot tea/coffee, a snack, and a box of tissues. This book is undoubtedly destined to be a light in a dark place for those still ashamed of their struggles. As you read, pull back the curtain of your heart and let the light of Jesus' presence shine and drive the darkness of sin away.

Acknowledgments

First, I thank God for the precious privilege of having another chance to share His incredible love for His people created in His image. God commissioned me to release a word of truth to bring knowledge and healing. Hosea states, ***"we are destroyed for lack of knowledge,"***

To my Father in the Lord, Bishop Enoch, your unfailing love throughout my life is unexplainable. Your sacrifice enabled me to dedicate my life again to my first love, Jesus Christ and restored the call upon my life.

I would also like to thank my "Reviving Souls Family" for working diligently behind the scenes. You covered all bases helping to fulfill the vision of this project. Your belief in the call on my life outside the church walls encouraged me to expand, reaching other audiences.

To my media team, Antonio and Tammie, your ideas for presentations were superb. To my stylist, Tramesa, for making amazing wardrobe choices and words of wisdom.

Janet, your expertise and how you made my story come alive was superb.

I would also like to thank Overseer Joseph, my brother Richard, family, and friends who covered me in prayer adding to my ability to conquer the roadblocks; I would not have completed this project without your perseverance.

And to all of you who purchased my first book and waited patiently for the sequel, I thank you!

Introduction

My name is Kamia, and this is my story of being born gay.

One of the most complex challenges in life is to forgive yourself for bad decisions and regain the trust of your family, church, and peers. I must admit forgiving myself was a difficult choice. Forgiving yourself means you are ready to move forward in life, and if you are Christian, realigning your life with God.

My soul needed healing from sin, low self-esteem, and the opinions of others who made no difference in my life. I forged ahead, not fully knowing how to embrace this much-needed place in my life.

You see, restoration is not like taking a pill for pain; after a couple of hours, you are good to go. I would soon find out it was a process that required an overhaul in my thoughts, familiar places, and adjusting to new relationships that strengthened my soul. After minutes, days, and months I started experiencing a new vibrant awakening that only comes from God. Once again, the God 'Mother White' constantly applauded created a newborn version of me.

My brokenness transformed into a place of wholeness, and my spirit took charge and led me to my next journey. While navigating my path, I would encounter long life lessons that strategically gave me wisdom.

My parents' role in my life was so vast that I don't have words to describe their contributions adequately. They were there from the beginning through the good, the bad, and the ugly. Some parents would have given up on their child, but not Clinton and Maxine; they held me close until I sorted the direction for my life as an adult. I tell you right now; if they had given up on me, I would have acted out on the thought of suicide. Suicide had me wrapped in its clutches and waking up in the morning, looming during lunch, tossing, and turning, trying to sleep at night.

God's path took me back to where I left off. He drew me through my love for music and His Presence. For since I can remember, I have been fascinated by music and the move of God. He re-introduced the choir from back in the day, and I found myself surrendering to the call of ministry again. I fell in love with God all over again, so how could I not obey His will.

Life was good, and I finally felt free to be me without the guilt and shame chained to me like a heavyweight. Everyone could see the old 'church girl' was back. I traveled, played music, and preached; it kept me busy and my mind off my past.

My forecast of life started changing. I had never thought about what it would be like to lose a parent. I watched others experience loss, and it always touched me deeply. Although God had prepared me through a vision, my emotions robbed me of my focus; I would plummet and have an 'Entanglement' experience. I wanted the thing that was bad for my soul. Was it true 'once gay, always gay?' The derailment caused immeasurable pain, and I found myself back in a place of darkness needing healing.

Clinton and Maxine were fixtures in my life, and I envisioned them being with me forever. The sacrifices they made for my success were selfless. Parents should desire to see their offspring moving forward in life, helping them recover from bad choices, mistakes, and embarrassing moments. Now my parents were superheroes, and not once did they fail me. Their love was infectious and continues to wrap me like a blanket until today. God has kept the promise of holding me up, keeping me steady, and providing for me since their departure. And for that, I Love Him.

God never forgets the assignment He has given us to fulfill. Somehow, I thought I would get a pass when it came to obeying the word of wisdom shared by Bishop, who was also my Father in the Lord. A few years after I reconciled with the Lord, he startled me by declaring God called me to lead a church. Who me? My response was I wouldn't pastor ten roaches with an extra-strength can of Raid. We both laughed as if we were at a comedy club! Suddenly, you could hear a pin drop, and Bishop said, "when God is ready, He will reveal it to you."

A few years later, God used a challenging situation to help me seek direction. The answer I received while prostrate on the floor floored me. Out of all the things that crossed my mind, I never thought; He would say, "I called you to be a senior leader." Later on, I would submit and establish Reviving Souls Ministries, Inc. in 2005.

I began to follow God's heart, and we experienced great moves of God. There was one subject He never stopped bringing before me. You see, God loves the LGBTQ community and those who were part of the 'don't ask, don't tell' churchgoers, despite the opinions of others. At one time in my life, I identified as a lesbian and felt that was part of my journey, and I honestly questioned that mindset again after the entanglement happened.

The Lord began preparing me to host events that taught about sexual perversion. You are correct if you guessed it was not a church's most popular plan of action. I realized that after twenty years, the church as I knew it remained silent on the subject.

A few years later, while praying, God spoke more concretely about the truths about being born gay, which made perfect sense. Although I understood that many would not be open to hearing or giving it thought, I accepted the responsibility to expose God's Heart about the matter. Souls are at stake, and I have the task to shift the pendulum giving others the freedom to be who God has positioned them.

Chapter 1

Chapter 1
Starting Over

Being away from God and His house had impacted me significantly. Although I had surrendered my life to the Lord again, I still felt like an outcast. I felt like a fish out of water would be the best way to describe the tightness I experienced in my chest every time I got out of my car and made the short walk up the sidewalk to the church door. My parents and Father in the Lord were pleased with my return to the fold, and I was also relieved and happy to be back where I knew I belonged.

My life had been a crazy rollercoaster ride over the past few years, and I was still struggling to overcome all the jostling and shaking around I had taken while on that ride. Fighting to become a person outside of God's design was exhausting, and I didn't realize just how tired my mind and emotions had grown throughout the ups and downs of the life I was trying to live. Like an old dried-out and stained dishrag, I felt used up, and in need of all the resurgence I could get.

But God was faithful to all my needs. Seeking the presence of God on a personal level was where I found the most comfort. It was just God and me! There was no need to wrestle with shame or guilt when I was before Him. God overwhelmed me, and the residue of guilt from my past finally lost its grip on me. The more I soaked in God, the more my heart and mind strengthened. I knew the recovery process was up to God; I had only to pursue Him. The truth was that I had gone hard after what I desired during those years that I had left God. I used no restraint when making choices. I took full advantage of walking out my feelings and my desires. I had lived my life for me and me alone. Now, I was going after God with even more passion. With love for Him and my gratitude for the mercy, He had shown toward me while I was operating outside His will, I was in hot pursuit of Him.

Worshipping with Mom was fulfilling, and I was so happy that she was no longer worried about me and my relationship with God. I guess I hadn't given much thought to what she had gone through as she tried to make sure her family knew the Savior. By this time, my father had said yes to Jesus as well. He had stopped partying, he no longer drank, and God had miraculously delivered him from the snare of adultery. Whew! Mother White's prayer life was speaking volumes. Her continuous laboring for our souls had finally paid off! It was a relief for her to have her husband and child attend church. She glowed with the joy that came with knowing that her family would spend eternity praising God. I'd never seen her cry more tears of joy or heard her praise louder.

I applauded the strength of my Father in the Lord, inviting me to come back as his musician. Saying yes to his invitation was a way for me to show my commitment to the house of God. While serving as the drummer, I cried many tears as God repaired my fragile heart. I represented the minority of those attending church. My brokenness screamed out loud every Sunday, but I was convinced this was my path.

For the most part, the church members didn't know the history of my ministry, and that was cool with me. At this point, I just wanted to be saved. The truth is, I told the Lord I never wanted to preach again. Playing the drums was okay, but that was the extent of my willingness to use my gifts. The last thing I wanted to do was go back to what I believed had caused me such great pain. Standing before the people, prophesying, and proclaiming the word of God, was what I wanted to give up altogether. I didn't feel worthy of the gift, and I was more than content to live without the weight of that mantle.

Mom would occasionally mention something about me preaching. Deep in my heart, I knew that she wanted me to teach again, and she was praying for the day that God would be ready for me to take up that mantle again.

Not me; I had no interest in returning to the pulpit. I had convinced myself that God had replaced me with somebody with far fewer issues than I had, and He no longer required me to do it anymore. I continued to concentrate on my healing and checked my heart for clutter. While I was out in the world, I had forgotten the feeling of having peace when I laid down at night. Finally, the arguing had ceased, I no longer laid awake at night trying to figure out what my next move should be, and I had even managed to break the habit of spending excess money. I had found that peace again, and I wasn't willing to sacrifice it.

Several months passed, and I was feeling competent and more emotionally sound. My thoughts became crystal clear as I wondered what my future would hold. Coming home every evening, spending quality time with my parents after a long day at work, and attending church as a family was enough for me. I realized just how much I had missed

15

them. Although I saw my parents every day while I was out in the world, there wasn't much quality to the time we spent together unless I was out of town. Mom and Dad made sure we often traveled to Georgia to visit family growing up. They also made sure we went to our favorite theme park for a weekend every summer. Being an only child, it wasn't unusual to spend a great deal of time with my parents. I felt like we were always having a family reunion, just the three of us!

While continuing the process of accepting my restoration, fellowshipping with my home church was comfortable. The thought of visiting other churches was another story, and it just seemed like a complete setup for a bad experience. My imagination would begin to tear down my newly developing confidence as soon as I found out our church received and accepted a letter to fellowship. I imagined how everyone would lean over to their neighbor to whisper about me as I walked down the aisle. The thought of it was almost crippling for me. But Mom would occasionally visit other venues and churches, and she needed me to come along with her to make sure she didn't lose her balance while walking in those unfamiliar places. Sometimes, we used a walker or wheelchair for her, which was always a great help. While it meant she could go where she wanted to without fear of falling, it also told me that I could use her need for assistance as a shield or distraction. I hoped that everyone would focus their attention on the devotion and determination my mother represented and not even notice that I was there.

I'd seen my mom needing help to secure her steps many times. So, making sure she could maneuver safely wasn't anything new for me. I had always admired my mom's fight to keep her agility. Soon after I decided to come back to God, Mom retired from the education system. That was a great move for her after the thirty years she had dedicated to the education of other people's children. She would no longer struggle to get up early every morning to prepare for work while in excruciating pain. Dad was already retired from work due to the complications he experienced due to seizures. Now, they would enjoy life together as a retired couple. I was so happy for them! They had both worked for many years, and it seemed to be a much-deserved bonus for them to spend their later years together.

One day, a friend invited me to attend a revival service held at her local church. I was apprehensive, but I knew I would eventually need to face the church people. My reasoning and reluctance weren't because I was ashamed; I just wasn't so sure what my response would be if approached incorrectly by some of the "saints." My soul had had more than enough of being ridiculed and treated as if God didn't love me. Before leaving the house that night, I said to God, "Now, keep your children's mouths closed if you want this to go smoothly. Because if not, it won't turn out so well!"

I intentionally arrived late to the revival service. Taking a seat in the very back of the church was good enough for me, and I didn't have to worry about everybody leaning over to whisper as I walked by them. By the time I got there, they were getting ready to introduce the speaker for the night. The guest preacher began to preach to the crowd, but at the same time, he was killing them with condemning statements. His words were hitting me like bullets! I said to God, "He is preaching straight condemnation!"

Now, I never expected the response I received from God. His voice clearly said, *"At least the preacher is trying to do what I called him to do!"*

My heart sank as I tried to wrap my mind around the reprimand. WOW! God had just shut my mouth because I had not been pliable in all areas. I wasn't serving Him at total capacity. I left the church that night looking like a deer in headlights. Boy, that was a long ride home! My mind was all over the place. I was convicted but not condemned. It seemed as if God's words had kidnapped my soul. For days I tried to shake His words, but nothing helped. I got up with those words every morning, and I went to sleep every night hearing them. The tables had turned on me. I felt like I was, once again, running from God. There were so many questions that needed answers. The questions were, HOW? WHAT? WHERE? And was there an audience?

I kept to myself the words God had spoken to me. He confronted me, and now I felt obligated to say yes to His Will. Moving forward, this would be one of the most challenging decisions in my life, and this was going to take a tremendous amount of courage and a level of confidence I had never had.

I couldn't believe I was even contemplating doing public ministry again. I was comfortable playing music; preaching was somewhere on a permanent vacation. The struggle to follow God while doing ministry was nothing I missed. I remained an intercessor, and I was still privately using my gift as a Seer. In my mind, returning to the pulpit wasn't an option.

One evening, while in prayer, I heard God's voice say, *"You will not meet Me in peace if you refuse to obey*

18

My will for your life." I failed God in the past, but I always recognized His voice.

With tears in my eyes, I said yes, I would obey. I admit there was a war going on in my soul. But my love for God had won, and I submitted to His will.

I remained in prayer about the proper timing to allow God to revive what He had started in me during my later teenage years. The thought of doing ministry again presented a war of doubt for me. I couldn't imagine anyone wanting to hear what a fallen preacher had to say. I questioned if I still had a word from God. Would it even be accepted? Was it really God's plan for me to become spiritually employed as a voice, or was it just my idea? I needed confirmation.

The most critical phase for me was to share my heart, surrendering my will to God with Mother White. Oh, the joy that hit my mother was great to watch! As soon as I told her, she began to lift her hands and dance around the kitchen! I knew she had been putting in some long and hard hours in prayer to push me to complete obedience. Even if it meant turmoil for me, I always wanted to please Mother White. I knew she wanted God's design for my life, and I also knew she prepared to defend her child's right to follow God.

I can't forget my dad. He was also happy and relieved to see me back in church, and he was more reserved with quiet joy. Honestly, I don't think he cared whether I returned to the pulpit or not. As long as I'd stopped running the streets, he was satisfied.

My mind was jumping from one thing to another, trying to figure out how God would work His plan. Even though I couldn't see it, I remained confident that He would accomplish what He set out to do. Little did I know, God was getting ready to take me back to a familiar place, a place where I was comfortable being who God had made me while using my gifts and talents.

One evening, I received a call from an old friend who had gone to college, graduated, and decided to return home and reside locally. Singing and directing choirs was a gift he used while growing up in the church. Although he was just an adolescent during the years of the first Community Choir, he never forgot how God was with the choir. One evening, he asked me if I thought our choir's founder and members would be interested in coming together again as a fully functioning choir. Listen, just thinking about that possibility was music to my ears! Having the chance to minister in song, travel to other events, and form great friendships again was what my soul needed. I knew how much my Father in the Lord had missed the choir he had founded. I could only hope and pray his answer to the idea of reviving the group would be yes, and I prayed he wanted that just as much as I felt like I needed it.

A few days later, my friend informed me that the Community Choir would relaunch under his direction, with my Father in the Lord as the Overseer and my mom as the faithful 'Choir Mom.' There were quite a few of us who were part of the old choir who were still in the area. Man, you could feel the excitement in the air as we planned and made arrangements to come back together. Most of us were only participating in the music departments at our respective churches, and some were doing nothing at all, not even attending a church. So, this was an opportunity for many new and returning choir members to rekindle their relationship with God. Music has a way of drawing us closer to Jesus.

At our first meeting, joy filled the room and anticipation! The truth is that most of us had become bored. There's always a natural desire to use your talents and gifts, and the average person is never happy to put those gifts on the shelf for long. Singing with the choir spoke to the evangelistic call we fulfilled. We had not forgotten how God touched the hearts of the audiences who came to hear us, minister.

Once the meeting convened, we decided on officers, uniforms, the rehearsal schedule, and the membership dues. Consumed with the choir's administration, we spent the rest of the night catching up with each other. We were okay with that, and we were just excited to be with others who had also chosen again to become part of something we all loved to do.

The news of the relaunch of the Community Choir quickly spread, and many gifted singers and musicians joined us. The choir's membership included two keyboardists, a saxophonist, four drummers, including myself, the sopranos, altos, and the tenors. The goals of the choir have not changed since its inception. Our number one goal was to bring others to Jesus while encouraging them to strengthen their relationship with Him. We welcomed the unsaved to be part of what we believed to be a life-altering experience. History began to repeat itself, as many unsaved members eventually came to Christ. I now began to understand the mind of God concerning me starting in ministry again, and he would use the choir as a common platform to heal my doubt.

When asked to pray for others, I couldn't say no. I realized I hadn't lost my passion for winning souls or seeing the broken restored during this time. Mother White witnessed the transformation I was going through as she traveled with the choir to local events. She was so happy to see us coming together, praying, and praising. God has a way of arranging events that lead to our obedience.

Before I knew it, an entire year had passed. Twelve months of healing and strengthening my relationship with God had brought me to this point. My life felt like it had finally reset, and I was moving in the right direction.

Along with doing ministry in the choir, God was still dealing with me in night visions. One night, God showed me a scene while sleeping. This time, what I saw involved my dad. Mom and I received a call from the hospital saying Dad had died. As soon as I hung up the phone, my dad walked into the bedroom and said, "I love you and your mama." He was calm, and he looked flawlessly unharmed. Dad walked over, hugged us, and made sure that we understood he had made it to Heaven. His last words to us were, "I love you both!"

Oh, my goodness! I woke up sweating, and my heart seemed to be beating a hundred beats per minute. In past times, God had dealt with me concerning the death of saints and other family members. But this time was entirely different for me. I knew that God was preparing me for the day He would call my father home.

Immediately, I began to pray for my dad, my mom, and myself. I used discretion and decided it was best not to share what the Lord had shown me with my mother. I didn't think she would be able to handle that particular revelation.

The last five years had been great for Mom and Dad. Like newlyweds, they enjoyed their life together at home, out to dinner, and traveling to their favorite place, Waycross. Dad had finally come to a place of surrendering his life to God, and he was seeing the value of a good wife. Our good times together continued, but I never forgot what God had shown me. I continued to pray and watch over my parents. I did whatever I could to make sure laughter and good times were always part of our lives. God had done what He promised. My family and I were experiencing love and great times together.

While enjoying my family, the choir experienced exponential growth; I gained more confidence in God's call upon my life. Restoration had come full circle for me! The bitterness against the church and my betrayers had melted away as I cried out to God. I no longer struggled with what my life was going to be like as I renewed my dedication to the ministry of the Gospel. A peace overwhelmed me, and I began to rest in God.

Playing and traveling with the choir became the highlight of my life. Every weekend we sang somewhere having a great time. It was as if it took up my idle time, and it helped me keep my heart clear from the hurt of my past. We always had a plan that consisted of the music we would do that night during rehearsals. Our agendas were never in stone, but we used our time wisely. There were nights the Holy Spirit would overshadow us during our practices. Sometimes, the Holy Spirit moved on us so powerfully we could no longer sing. We worshiped and allowed God to visit us; on some occasions, the Lord would prompt me to prophesy during the visitation. We weren't perfect, by any means, but the presence of God often engulfed us as a reminder that He was indeed the "author and the finisher of our faith."

At one point, we received an invitation to sing in Alabama. That night, as we prepared for the concert, the Holy Spirit came in like a mighty, rushing wind! The Lord gave me a message for the choir. The word of the Lord was, "Do not expect a monetary blessing from this trip, but it will be a spiritual blessing because of your sacrifice!"

Most of us were weeping uncontrollably. I had no idea what God was saying, but I trusted that He would manifest the meaning when we returned home. While traveling back, we stopped by a church. The church was small in attendance due to a state convention. Most of their parishioners attended the state meet, so there was plenty of room for us to join them in the sanctuary. They were so glad we stopped in and worshipped with them. We ministered in song, and my Father in the Lord preached the house down! They were so appreciative, and without having to ask for anything, they gave us everything they could out of their kitchen. We got back in the vans with potato chips, cookies, and Chek drinks bags! They must have emptied their Sunday School snack stash for us. They gave an offering to help us travel home, and we were grateful.

After returning from Alabama, we rested the following Monday. Everyone was excited to return to rehearsal to discuss the highs and the lows of the trip. We arrived home, only to discover that some of the choir members were suffering from food poisoning. Even still, the wins outweighed the low moments.

We came together two weeks later for rehearsal. As always, we opened practice with prayer and worship. Most of

24

us had forgotten what God had promised us as a gift for our obedience and sacrifice. An unusual 'Presence of God' began to fill the room as we worshipped. The power of the Holy Spirit arrested our plans. I started hearing instructions to pray for each member of the choir. The Presence of God was so heavy in the room that most of the choir members could not stand as I touched them. Some shook under the power of God, and some received their prayer language. It was as if God was running a personal revival for the choir.

We stayed longer that night because so many of us were under the influence of the Holy Spirit. They were unable to drive home right away safely. When I finally arrived home, there were no words to adequately describe how the Presence of the Lord had swept through the room. What just happened, and why was I instructed to pray for everyone and encourage them to surrender to God! He reminded me of the promise He'd made through the prophecy. A refreshing, renewal, and infilling of the Holy Spirit was the promise. God had selected me to pray for those who desired more of Him.

Word of how miraculously the Presence of the Lord manifested at that rehearsal went out quickly among the choir members. During that time, my cousin and friend, along with her children, stayed with me. The Holy Spirit filled my godbrother and his little sister. I could hardly believe what I was witnessing; a ten and nine-year-old speaking in tongues.

I walked next door to my parent's house and tried to explain what had just happened in rehearsal. My aunt was there visiting with my parents. She had been a member of the original Community Choir. She became so excited as I tried to describe the night's events she asked if I would pray for her. I told her that I couldn't promise God would move as He had in rehearsal, but I would certainly pray for her. Much to my surprise, my aunt couldn't stand under the power of God. She began to speak in an unknown tongue. I was in total shock; unexplainable things were happening! When she could, my aunt got up off the floor, touched my dad, and he hit the floor, praising God! Whew!

I was trying to figure out if this was just for that night or the choir members. Before going to bed, I decided to pray, but all I could do was praise God and speak in tongues. I was filled with His Spirit too, and my cup ran over. Filled with God's Presence, my little godbrother was crying and speaking in tongues, nonstop. I could only sit in awe of what God was doing, which was unique. Finally, I said, "He can't sleep like this!" God then instructed me to touch him; he immediately passed out and fell asleep in my bed. I tossed and turned all night. My spirit felt like it was running, and I could only catch cat naps that night.

My phone rang off the hook after that Monday night, and I couldn't say what had happened. The next day, I arrived at work, and all day, my mind replayed the images and sounds of the past evening. It seemed as if it was a dream. In all my years, there's never been a time I witnessed the weight of God's presence consume others with such might. Most of those who were present would agree that this was their first encounter with God's glory manifesting in this manner. In my early years of ministry, I'd prayed for some people, and they would fall under God's power. But this was something new for me, and I was truly baffled!

As soon as work was over, I headed home. My physical body was a little tired from not sleeping the night before. While unlocking my front door, I could hear my phone ringing and ringing. While I was trying to put my things down and catch my breath, I missed the call. Five minutes later, the phone rang again. I answered the phone, and a choir member who missed the previous night's rehearsal wanted to come to my house to receive prayer. She was so excited, and she wanted to have the same experience she'd heard about from those who were with me the night before. My response was, "Sure! But I can't promise you God will show up like He did last night." She said she understood that, but she still wanted me to pray with her.

The doorbell rang about seven o'clock that evening. My cousin was with me, and she had already received the Holy Spirit's outpouring the night before. I opened the door, feeling awkward because I didn't know how to get started. Everything had happened so fast the night before, and I couldn't recall what had been the trigger. Suddenly, I heard God's voice of instruction very clearly, almost scaring me. The directions were to start with prayer and praise God with our voices and handclaps. I began to lead us in worship and praise. The more we praised God, the more we began to feel the power of His presence filling the room. We shouted, "Yes, Lord, repeatedly to the top of our lungs." The Holy Spirit began to move as it had the night before.

My experience with being a Pentecostal included shouting, speaking in tongues, and sometimes rolling on the floor while under the power of God. So, to be part of a great move of God wasn't foreign to me. But God did a new thing that night! The choir member I was praying with began to laugh uncontrollably, and we literally had to hold her up while she praised God in between laughing. My cousin and I were stunned, and neither of us had ever seen that before.

Time wasn't of the essence, but I noticed it was already eleven o'clock. Oh my God! We had experienced such an outpouring and overflow of the Holy Spirit that we had lost track of time. Immediately, I started to wonder how our choir member would get home. My cousin and I decided that it would be best to take her home because she was too drunk in the spirit to drive. My other concern was how her mom would accept her daughter's reaction to God's power.

We drove across town to the young lady's home. After knocking at the door, her mother came to the door. I recognized all mothers' concerns when a late-night knock is at the door, and their child isn't home. I quickly tried to explain that the presence of God had moved on her daughter, and we were sorry we didn't realize the time. I assured her that, while it looked like her daughter had been drinking, she was sober, just under the influence of the Holy Spirit. The mother looked at her daughter's condition, noting that she couldn't stand or walk independently, and she continued to laugh loudly. The look on her mother's face told me that she didn't believe me or approve of what was going on. She motioned for us to take her daughter to her bedroom. We began to walk towards the room so she could lay down.

As we were helping her get to bed, something else unusual happened. God's power touched her like fire before we could put her on the bed, and she began to speak in an unknown tongue! The Holy Spirit was so strong until all three of us, including the girl's mother, could no longer stand. I'd never felt the power of God to that magnitude while witnessing a person filled with God's spirit. I thought I had been amazed the night before, but this was on a new scale! My cousin and I rode home in complete silence, only occasionally whispering praise to God.

28

The following day, I concluded that God was granting an outpouring of His spirit to everyone who desired it. Later that day, I received another phone call from a choir member who wanted to experience the presence of God. I set a time to meet with them and waited for God's directives. This time, the instructions were more direct. The Lord required that those who had come to experience His power stand on a specific spot after I prayed with them. In my mind, I was wondering, "*What in the world is happening now!*" I knew I had to obey despite my curiosity to receive my blessings.

In obedience, I asked my visitors to stand in the spot God had indicated. We began to pray and then to praise. While standing on the 'God spot,' we watched the power of God move on our guests. Like before, they couldn't stand, and they fell out praising God while their bodies shook under His touch. After about an hour of praise, the Holy Spirit filled them, and they began to speak in an unknown tongue.

Within three days, God had filled children and many adults with the Holy Spirit. God would continue to send church members and choir members to my house for encounters with His presence. One night, He sent a member oppressed by a demonic influence. After prayer, we followed the instructions given the previous nights. My guest stood on the 'God spot' and praised. The enemy began to reveal himself to us and vowed not to release the member from bondage. Earlier that day, I felt the urge to fast. I didn't quite understand why I needed to fast, but I did. Later, I understood that the fasting didn't move God, but it impacted my faith and increased my stamina. My guest began to weep as the enemy spoke through them, declaring that they belonged there. In Jesus' name, I said the guest's name and decreed their freedom through the blood of Christ.

The next set of instructions included half-filling a glass with water and adding oil I had prayed over. My guest drank the oil and water mixture, and within minutes, they were overwhelmed with the need to use the restroom. The demonic influence expelled, and freedom rang! I led them in a prayer of repentance, discussed iniquity with them, and encouraged them to remain in prayer even after that evening.

I had lost count of just how many people had experienced an encounter with the presence of God while they were in my home. A month went by, and one evening, I spoke with my dad about everything. I explained how God's power and His plan had utterly dumbfounded me. My dad listened closely to what I had to say. Then, he said, "Shot, I have a dream to share in his quiet way. I dreamed there was a steeple on top of your house, and it was on fire!"

Growing up into my adult life, I had never heard my dad discuss his dreams. So, I stood there shocked for a few seconds in anticipation. God showed my dad that my house had a steeple on it, and it was on fire! The dream explained everything that was taking place in my life. Could Dad have of also been a Seer, and we didn't know it. He had never shared dreams with Mom or me before.

God in His Divine wisdom had chosen me to be part of His plan to bring revival to those who wanted a more in-depth experience with Him. I couldn't explain or understand why He chose me. I had only been back in church a year, and I considered myself just a musician who was learning to submit all my gifts again. That conversation with my dad will always stay with me. It deeply moved me to hear my dad reveal God's then-present orders for my life. I then understood that it didn't matter how I viewed myself; God's will took precedence over those considerations for my life.

My everyday routine had changed, and my eating habits were no longer the same. My diet consisted of broth during the day and a small meal after the prayer gatherings. My workdays were filled with prayer as I went about my job, and the miracles continued to happen.

One of the choir members contracted the flu. It had become difficult for her to breathe and walk simultaneously. When she was at her absolute weakest point, she requested prayer for healing. I agreed to pray for her; at that point, my faith was at an all-time high. I believed that every person who desired more of God would receive more of him.

When guests would come to my house, asking for prayer, I would no longer touch them. I would ask them to stand on the 'God spot' on the carpet, and His power would saturate them without fail! This night, things were no different with my flu-infected choir member. She fell to her knees as she praised God, speaking in her prayer language.

I would always keep watchful during the encounters. Most participants would experience deep worship with God for about an hour. After her God encounter, she was on her knees; she reached up as if someone had grabbed her arms and rose from the floor. We watched in utter amazement! How was she able to get up from the floor with perfect balance? She had been so weak when she arrived an hour earlier. She later shared that she thought I had reached down and helped her get up. I quickly told her that I hadn't touched her. She explained that two hands reached for her when she looked up and effortlessly lifted her. By the time she prepared to leave my house, healing had occurred. Even her fever had broken. What a mighty God we serve! If I had any doubts about the power of God, they lifted that night.

31

This peculiar anointing had begun to operate outside of my home. There were people in my church who heard how God was touching the lives of others. After church, some members began to request prayer, and I wasn't comfortable doing that because we had just ended the church service and altar calls given by those in charge of the service. Out of respect, I asked my Father in the Lord if it would be appropriate for me to pray for those still requesting prayer, and he released me to pray.

As I prayed, God's glory continued to overpower everyone. The church members would leave me with the one who requested prayer, and God would minister to them. One thing about it, God never rushed anyone's time with Him. I witnessed others on the floor, shaking under the power of God for hours at a time.

After visiting other churches, a few of the participants from the prayer gatherings would go with me. After the services, we'd often return to my house, and I'd cook a quick meal for us. On one of those occasions, as we were traveling home, one of the men in the group said he felt strange. He described it as a movement in his belly. He said there wasn't any pain, just unusual motion. Immediately, the Holy Spirit told me that this young man was about to birth his prayer language. We had to skip our trip to the store and make a beeline for the house. By the time I pulled my car into the driveway, the presence of God was taking him over entirely. I jumped out from behind the steering wheel, ran to unlock the front door, and then returned to the car to help get him out of the back seat. While rushing to help get him across the threshold, the Holy Spirit touched, releasing tongues. Again, the power of his new language, accompanied by a 'mighty rushing wind,' pushed us all to our knees. Up until that point, I'd heard all my instructions in an audible voice, but God had a new thing to introduce that night.

As I looked at my carpet, it appeared to be moving like the waves on the ocean. I said to myself, "This is too much! Lord, what are you doing!" I questioned the others, and they testified that they also saw the carpet move as we sat. God had opened our spiritual eyes, and he wanted to reveal His sovereignty, and we were on holy ground.

Mom's heart filled with joy as she watched her baby striving to follow God. The signs and miracles that manifested felt much like the book of Acts. I was happy that some of the members of my church had the opportunity to encounter the Holy Spirit. Some of them even received from the Lord standing beside their vehicle. I believe God gave everyone who asked for it a measure of His spirit. All the preliminary things we took people through in the church gatherings were no longer part of the process God used. He was looking for a 'yes' in their souls.

I saw and encountered God in a way that I had never encountered Him before. One of the sisters who traveled from a nearby city said, "God has called you to be a Pastor." I was left wondering why she would say such a thing? Of course, I dismissed her proclamation. I wasn't interested in pastoring anybody. I wanted to serve my Father in the Lord, doing whatever I could to help bring his vision to fruition.

After about three months and countless souls filled with the spirit, God seemed to stop the unique flow of His presence. You see, I had always loved the Spirit of God and how it moved to bless others. So, coming to terms with God's decision to move on from the unusual 'wind of His spirit' saddened me greatly. I was inquiring of God concerning His sovereignty; questioning God never used to be an option. But I decided to take a chance and ask God why He had discontinued the rare form of outpouring? Hadn't I been obedient to His leading?

God's answer to my questions left me speechless! He said, *"Those in your fellowship opposed Me; they didn't want Me if it came through you! He said, "I choose to forgive and empower man using them at my discretion; they didn't want me because I wanted you."*

Tears rolled down my face. I was comforted only by the realization that I had not displeased the Lord, but I can't lie and say that I wasn't disturbed by the hearts of others. The spirit of rejection worked hard to take me back to the place I had left before. Recognizing the trap of walking in my emotions, I isolated myself in prayer, seeing only my parents. I refused to succumb to the cries of rejection in my life again.

Chapter 2

Chapter 2
Recommitted to the Call

The choir continued to experience God's Presence as we traveled to various events. I continue to be grateful for the humility in which my Father in the Lord served God and others throughout that time. He taught us to minister in humility and gratitude and with confidence in our abilities and the calling God had placed on our lives.

I'll never forget when we received an invitation to minister as part of a musical at an out-of-town church. We were the last choir to sing, but we had no problem supporting the six or seven ensembles called to the choir stand before us. Before we took the choir took the stand, you felt the presence of God in the atmosphere. The whole church broke into praise while we sang "They That Wait Upon the Lord." Like thunder, the sound of shouting and handclaps filled the room as we poured out our praise before the Lord. We gladly gave everything we had, and it was well-received.

Later that night, as we prepared to travel home, I was stopped by one of the church attendees who said, "You guys won!" Astonished by his comment, we assured him we didn't come to compete and that everybody who took part in the program was singing their hearts out. We received so many positive comments as we made our way back to the vans to leave. I'm still surprised by some of the things people said about us. It's always good to know that the offering of your gifts and talents has blessed someone.

We were always starving after a service or program. On our way home, there was usually a lot of laughing, singing, and discussion about the things we did well, ways we could improve our ministry, and how far away we were from the closest McDonald's. After a program, eating at McDonald's was just an unspoken part of our routine. We shared our food and our money with each other, and there was never a time that we came back home without being spiritually and physically filled.

I was always excited to have a chance to exercise my faith while ministering to others. Mom was president of the women's ministry. Every third Sunday, she would moderate the service. Part of her responsibility was to choose a speaker for those Sundays. I knew Mom was entertaining the idea of me returning to the pulpit. Eventually, she asked me to share my testimony during one of those third Sunday services. It would be the first time I'd publicly speak about my past failures and triumphs. As I prepared my message for that Sunday, I was very nervous, wondering if the judgments against me would increase. I understood that most people kept their failures and missteps private for fear of becoming outcasts, even though it was their past. I knew that some churchgoers have no problem omitting God's mercy and grace related to others. I had witnessed some given another chance to start over, while others shunned for their actions. Sometimes, it depended on who they were, who they knew, or how their mishaps came to light. If you were fortunate enough to receive that second chance, you could return to the fold and not face unrelenting judgment. Once guilty, always guilty!

The Sunday that was set aside for me to share my testimony of God's love and grace toward me was quickly approaching. Mom had only told my Father in the Lord that I would be speaking, and she wasn't going to give anyone a chance to ruin my confidence before I even had an opportunity to get started. She knew my Father in the Lord would only speak words of encouragement to me, and he would be praying with me and for me as I prepared to face the Saints.

Visitors were worshipping with us that third Sunday. It was a complete surprise to the audience when my mom introduced me as the speaker sharing my story. As I stood firmly before the audience, my insides shook violently with fear. My palms began to sweat, and my mouth became desert dry, but I knew God was there with me despite how I felt. As I ran my eyes over the faces in the audience, I realized that most of them had only known me as a drummer, nothing else. Speaking about my experiences and God, getting up before that crowd seemed so far beyond my abilities.

I whispered an internal prayer, glanced down at my notes, grabbed the sides of the pulpit to steady my shaking hands, and finally began speaking. At first, my voice didn't even sound like my own. I cleared my throat, licked my dry lips, and started again. While speaking, I kept my eyes fixed on the one person, Mom, who believed in me. I focused on the face of my cheerleader, Mom. I knew if I could just see her face, full of compassion and approval, that would be enough to keep me going until I felt secure enough to look down at my notes and then look up again and engage my audience. She smiled and gave me several little, almost unnoticeable nods. It was just what I needed.

After about ten minutes of speaking, I felt the atmosphere shift. The Holy Spirit permeated the room. Every opposition was blocked, commanding victory for God's glory! Before the service began, Mom had urged me to appeal to those who desired prayer after sharing my testimony. I did that, and there was a great response to my surprise. People came forward from every corner of the room. Some of them even opened up and shared personal downfalls in the area of sexual perversion. They were encouraged to know that others had experienced the same failures, but they were now winning the battle.

When I finally arrived home after church, I collapsed from the emotional exhaustion of holding my breath for days while you prepare to put yourself out there the way I had. I felt like a freight train had hit me head-on, and it was all I could do to stumble from my car and make it into the house. It took about two hours before I felt exuberant again. I finally had enough energy to reflect on the whole thing. It suddenly came to me that my dad had also had a chance to hear me tell my story. Hearing him say that he was proud of his baby spoke volumes to my self-esteem. It had been two years since I had been relieved of the weight of depression and bitterness. Finally, I could feel the burden of unforgiveness and resentment fleeing from my heart; I wore its residue like a badge of honor. It felt so good to have put those weights aside with God's help. My heart was finally light.

Things continued to get better for me. Despite the rollercoaster of my personal life, I continued to display a good work ethic on my job. I enjoyed managing people and providing excellent customer service. Our store manager was a hard-working team player, and she was fair and knowledgeable about soft-lines and hard-lines. There was an open position for a manager in one of the soft-line departments, but I never interviewed for the job, and I didn't have the confidence to put my hat in the ring.

While the store manager was on vacation, I had a night vision. In that vision, the manager promoted me to the open position. I understood that the manifestation could happen right away or in the future. Another employee had applied for the job, and she was more experienced than I was. It didn't matter; God had intended for me to have that current position upon my manager's return. The following week, I sat in my manager's office, interviewing for the job. I had the least amount of experience, but it was God's choice for the promotion. That carries more weight than all the experience in the world. A few days later, she awarded me the manager's position.

During the summer, I liked taking my vacations. Sometimes, Mom and Dad would travel to Waycross, and I would meet them there. After checking my time, I discovered that I had accumulated over two weeks of leave. While making plans to get away, the Holy Spirit spoke to me and said, *"Take your parents to Waycross and spend ten days with them."*

These were new instructions for me. I didn't question God; I told my parents to pack their bags. We were going to Waycross for two weeks. I hadn't seen them that excited since I gave my heart back to Jesus! The idea that I was doing something that made my parents so happy brought me so much joy. It was nice to see them excitedly scurrying through the house, gathering suitcases, and frantically planning and discussing what they would be taking for two weeks. Dad left most of the packing and preparing to my mom while he focused on checking and double-checking the car's tires, brakes, and fluids. He took his family's traveling safety seriously. It was two-hundred and thirty-five miles to Waycross, and he didn't want any trouble while we were on the road.

While traveling to Waycross, Dad never wanted to stop for anything. That wasn't anything new. I remember being a little girl, traveling with my parents, and using a small bucket so Dad could drive straight through without stopping for me to use the restroom. On the other hand, Mom would plan a picnic ninety miles outside our destination. The night before we left, she would always put soda cans and water bottles in the freezer. The next day, those frozen solid cans and bottles would be put in a plastic bag and placed in the car. She would get up early before our departure, fry chicken wings, wrap them in aluminum foil, and put them in the car's back window. The sun kept the food hot and fresh while we were traveling. The smell of fried chicken and sun-warmed bread traveled with us, whetting my appetite and swaying me to take Mom's side in the discussions about whether to stop and eat.

What a plan Mom had for those rest-stops. Dad would be so angry until he sat on the other side of the picnic table, eating his perfectly seasoned, perfectly warmed chicken sandwich and drinking his thawed soda. Even though I knew he was secretly enjoying the food my mom had so lovingly prepared, the scowl on his face, without a shadow of a doubt, told us there would be no talking, no laughing, and no playing around. His goal was to eat quickly and get back on the road. His attitude didn't bother Mom one bit; it was nothing new to her. He could pout all he wanted; we were stopping to have a picnic!

For this trip to Waycross, I had no requests for Dad about our travel. I just made him promise to be on my schedule, not his. He understood that this meant he couldn't complain, even if we stopped to walk the avenues. Dad was a real trooper; he thoroughly enjoyed our time at the shopping venues and paid for our lunch at a pizza joint. Instead of our travel time being a couple of hours, it took us nine hours. Stopping to eat, look and shop added five hours to our travel time. It was amazing to see how much my dad had changed since I was a child. We had an incredible time together those two weeks in Waycross. I took my mom to see her first cousins who lived in the city of Naylor. She hadn't seen them in over thirty years! Wow! She had shared her memories with me on several occasions, so meeting them for the first time was heartfelt. I was sad to see our vacation time come to an end. The Lord knew just what I needed at that particular time.

Upon returning home, I had a few vacation days left. The bright idea that we needed to take new family pictures came to me. The last pictures we took showed me standing there with a then-popular Jheri curl! How many moons ago had that been! It was a stunning Jheri curl, always looking good and never dripping! Mom always got her hair professionally styled, and I would cut Dad's hair myself, what was left of it! As I looked at those old, outdated pictures, what I saw didn't represent who I was at that moment. New family pictures were a must. No more curls for me! My following picture would show me relaxed hair styling an asymmetrical haircut. We were beautiful and all cleaned up for our new pictures. God, the Great Potter, had put me back on the wheel. I was a new person in Christ, and I felt like that newness, and the pride, my parents, felt because of that newness, showed in our new family portrait.

My vacation was almost over, and I was soaking the last moments of napping on my couch. The Lord visited me and showed a nurse calling, saying, 'Mr. White passed away.'

Immediately I jumped up, breathing hard and not wanting to accept the Lord's vision. How could this be; our family was enjoying God and being together. Could God be talking about taking my dad right now? But why; Dad was living his best life. I decided not to share with Mom the vision feeling like it would be too much for her to consume. So, for months, I prayed for our family, too afraid to question God about what I saw.

Finally, I was back at work in my new position. The great thing about the company is that they chose you for the lead position based on your management skills. Having product knowledge wasn't a deal-breaker. But, having a person who could manage reports and numbers was essential. Learning the product could come later.

The employee who interviewed for the position and had more product knowledge experience than I did was now working for me. There was noticeable tension between us because of my lack of product knowledge. The whole situation reminded me of how Dad responded to a new position without knowing anything about the job. He signed up for the small engine mechanic's course at Brevard Community College. Because he was part of the union, it was mandatory to give him ninety days to gain the knowledge he needed for that job. Well, Dad passed the three-month course and mastered his new position. My takeaway from that was that I needed to be assertive about learning the product I was managing; it proved to be the best approach to finding a much-needed confidence level.

Visiting the library became a frequent pastime for me. I spent hours checking through books and watching videos explaining my product and how to sell it. It didn't take long for all those hours at the library to pay off for me. A few months later, the district manager visited my department. As he spoke and made suggestions on how to increase our productivity, I was able to comprehend all the work terminology and ask valid questions. The visit was a success, and I received praise for being a fast learner. Once the employee saw that I was knowledgeable and competent, the eye rolls stopped, and so did the sighs. But I always felt that she still believed she was a better choice. It was then that I realized that if God promotes you, it doesn't matter who disagrees with it.

The Lord was gracious to me during my time as a department manager. The district manager was grooming me to become a soft-line manager, and I was excited about taking on more responsibilities. But seemingly out of nowhere, God revisited me about my job one night while sleeping. In my vision, He showed me, my district manager, offering me a soft-line management position in another city. He complimented me on my work and told me he thought I'd do well in a new role.

The Lord wasted no time sharing the meaning of that night vision. He wanted me to be aware of my district manager's intentions, but His will for me was to remain in the city and care for my parents. A week later, I was surprised by an unannounced visit from the district manager. He seemed so excited to tell me about the available opportunity for promotion. As he started giving me the details about the position and congratulating me for my rapid climb within the company, I dropped my head so he wouldn't see the tears that welled up in my eyes. As soon as I felt like I could control my emotions, I raised my head, smiled, and thanked him wholeheartedly for considering me for the position. I explained why I couldn't take the job he offered, and I hoped he would understand my reasoning for not accepting what I had worked so hard to achieve. His gracious response made me feel like he wholeheartedly understood my loyalty to God and my parents' welfare. I hadn't always done a great job listening to God in past times, but I was determined to be obedient at all costs this time.

Mom and Dad would visit the doctor monthly for check-ups and bloodwork. Their doctor made adjustments in their medications according to the results of their previous tests. Both took prescribed medicines daily, helping them remain healthy. In October of 1998, my parents visited the doctor for the test results of the prior month, and those tests concluded that my dad was very sick.

After work, I had a routine I followed. I came in one evening screaming, "Where is everybody?" Mom and Dad were sitting in the kitchen. I couldn't put my finger on it, but something was terribly wrong. There was an unusual heaviness in the air. They spoke to me, but their usual laughter and greetings weren't the same. Dad's shoulders slumped downward, and I knew his posture indicated a burden. He asked me to sit at the bar with him and Mom. I was on pins and needles, wanting to hear and not wanting to know what was on their heart. I hadn't seen my parents so tense since the last time we received tragic news about a family member's unexpected death. It was like waiting for someone else to end their phone conversation so they could tell you why they kept saying 'Oh no!'.

Dad paused, quickly glanced at my mother, and explained their doctor's visit. I couldn't take my eyes off him. His demeanor and his posture kept my eyes glued to his face. Mom was quiet as she supported Dad with just her presence in the room. Dad continued talking, revealing the test results: cancer in the colon. The atmosphere no longer filled the usual greeting, and I could hardly breathe. I was devastated, but I did my best to hold it together for Mom and Dad. They would need me more than ever, and I had to show them that I could be strong support.

I began to drive my parents to their doctor's appointments from that point on. The doctor scheduled Dad for surgery and multiple rounds of chemo immediately following the surgery. I started making calls to family members, asking for prayer. We also notified our pastor, and he walked with us through the entire process. Dad never showed any signs of fear, but I knew he was thinking of Mom and me, wondering if he had done enough. He talked a lot about his faith in God, trusting Him to be with him.

A couple of days later, we arrived at the hospital for Dad's surgery. Mom and I prayed with him and watched them roll him away. It was a sad moment, but we took a seat in the waiting room and began talking and laughing enthusiastically. Thank God for settling our minds and giving us peace at that moment. A few hours later, the surgeon walked over to us and provided us with an evaluation of the outcome of Dad's surgery. He was confident that the surgery removed all cancer from Dad's colon and only needed chemo to remove any remaining undetected cancerous cells.

Excited to see Dad, we patiently waited for the nurses to bring him back to his room from recovery. He was resting when they rolled him into the room, but Dad opened his eyes and smiled at us after a few minutes. His smile eased any anxiety we may have been experiencing. We knew he would be trash talking at any minute, and we couldn't wait to hear it. That was going to be the sign that sealed the deal for me. It didn't take long before he turned his face toward my Mom and began his usual teasing her. We couldn't give God a 'crazy praise' because of the noise restrictions, but with hands raised, we gave Him a wave offering and a low-key "thank you!"

We remained with Dad for the rest of the day and late into the night. Finally, he convinced us that he was doing good, and we should go home and rest. Mom and I thanked God on the way home, clapping our hands and shouting to the rooftop with undignified praise! We knew if we had cut loose like that in the hospital, they would have checked us both into the mental ward for evaluation.

After a long day, Mom's body needed to rest from being so tense. She had fibromyalgia, which caused her chronic back pain. I knew she was uncomfortable sitting up for hours, but the pain wasn't going to interfere with her commitment to her husband. Convincing her to leave the hospital before she was satisfied that Dad was in good hands would never happen. She loved my dad with all her heart, through their bad days and the good days. She wasn't going to do anything differently now that he wasn't well.

After a well-rested night, we returned to the hospital to meet with the doctor again, as he was to determine a possible release date for Dad. That was good news; we'd missed having him at the house with us, and things just weren't the same without him. We visited the hospital twice every day, ensuring he knew we cared about him and loved him. Finally, the day came that Dad could go home from the hospital. I called those I knew who had prayed for the success of his surgery. Family and friends were thrilled with the update. I don't think I had ever seen Dad so enthusiastic about going to the house.

Dad saw his primary doctor shortly after his hospital release. The doctor seemed confident that the prescribed chemo treatments would add to the possibility of Dad's complete recovery. Dad's regiment of chemo treatments started the following week, three times a week. His doctor explained the possible side effects of receiving chemo; they were horrible. As he read off that terrible list of possible side effects, I tried my best not to look so concerned, making sure Dad saw only my faith. I had already heard that chemo was rough on the body. Hair loss, change in skin complexion, weight loss, and loss of appetite could result from chemo. There's no way to prepare yourself for that.

Coming straight home from work became the norm for me. I made sure I didn't do anything else before checking on my parents. My daily to-do list always included running their errands, picking up meals for dinner, and making sure Mom was always with Dad. I didn't want any extra strain placed on her. After Mom's diagnosis of chronic fibromyalgia, my aunt, Dad's sister started coming over to help maintain the house while I was at work. Every Friday night, Auntie would arrive at about seven o'clock. She knew Mom had stacks of chocolate waiting for her. Of course, you know we all helped her eat her chocolate! There was no way she could have eaten it all by herself. She never complained about being there, and it was apparent she had a deep love for her brother and sister-in-law.

Some days, after making sure my parents had everything they needed, I would go home, shower, and rest on my couch. One day, while lying there resting my mind, the Lord came to me again and showed me a clear vision. "I was wide awake on the couch, but I could see a brown casket with my dad, and he was dressed in a brown suit and surrounded by many flowers." The setting was at a local church that hosted many funerals. It was evident that God was getting me ready for His sovereign will. God gave no timeframe, so I hoped and prayed this was a couple of years down the road.

Mom took Dad to his first chemo appointment. I thought about him all day while I was at work, and I couldn't wait for my shift to end so I could check on him. I'm positive I was speeding as I made my way to my parent's house that evening. I unlocked their door and made a beeline to Dad's favorite chair. He blurted out, "Shot, how is Daddy's baby?" His words, and the energy with which he spoke, eased my mind.

I quickly answered, "I'm good if you are good!" He convinced me that everything had gone well that day, and he was in no pain. It was only then that I could exhale, and I felt like I had been holding my breath all day, waiting to see his face.

For the next two months, Dad endured the chemo, but I worried about its toll on his body. After two weeks of the treatments, visible wear and tear showed on Dad's skin. His skin tone became darker, and his nails changed color. Slowly he began to lose his appetite showing signs of fatigue, and he had noticeably lost weight. Although we were aware of the potential side effects of the treatments, emotionally, it was hard and sad to watch his body experience the physical changes.

During this time, my uncles and aunts were a great help. They would visit Dad during the day and assist Mom with taking care of him. Dad wasn't a complainer, and he insisted that he was doing alright, even when I could tell that he was having a rough day. My friends called and came by often to check on him and visit with him. Many of them knew him from when he would cook for the choir. I appreciated their love and concern for my family.

I counted down the weeks of chemo, waiting anxiously for the end. Dad was counting down as well. His body needed a break from the harsh treatments. Seeing him in that condition was a constant reminder of my vision of his death, and it began to loom large in my thoughts. I dismissed them and continued to pray for mercy, hoping God would add time to his life. I often saw the worry and concern on Mom's face. I strengthened myself to be a source of strength for her whenever she needed it. Mom had already witnessed the most incredible miracle when it came to Dad. The day he gave his life to Christ and joined the church was a constant reminder that God could do anything! No situation was too hard for Him!

Finally, after persevering, the two months of chemo treatments came to an end! With great anticipation, we waited for Dad's scheduled doctor's visit. We received the news we were praying for; the cancer was no longer a threat! Everything went well, and there was no need to worry. That was the best news I'd heard in a long time. I called my family who lived out of town, thanked them for their prayers, and updated them on Dad's health. I also thanked my church family and friends for their loyal prayers and visits. Although Dad had completed the treatments, he was still weak. But we knew good rest and some good down home-cooked food would lift his spirits and strengthen his body.

Two weeks later, Dad cracked jokes, thumped me on my knuckles, and cooked for his family. It had been three months since he was able to be himself. I can't describe how I felt hearing his laughter. The first Sunday came, and he was getting ready to praise his God and boy did Dad cut the rug dancing until there was no more strength left. His eyes filled with tears as he hugged my mom. What an unforgettable moment they experienced that day! In my mind, they were a picture of passion and praise clinched arm in arm! I sat on the pew, weeping before God. Only I knew how far God had brought my dad. I saw Mom cry a lot of nights to God over his soul.

In April, I received an invitation to preach a three-day revival. I hadn't preached three consecutive days before, so I was nervous. I prayed, and God answered that He orchestrated the event. After knowing that, I felt much more at ease to accept the invitation. Mom and Dad wanted to support me in my first endeavor as a revivalist by staying with me while I was out of town, and I was so excited to have them come along with me. My cousin also surprised me by traveling from Georgia to join me, and we all stayed in a hotel.

We arrived at the hotel midday that Wednesday got settled in, and then went to an early dinner. I kept telling myself that I would be alright, but fear was trying to talk louder than I was. Sometimes you just must 'clap back' and believe what you tell yourself. As soon as we walked into the church, we felt tremendous love. The audience was familiar, and we had fellowshipped together in the past. That was a great help! They were genuinely glad to see that I had returned to my walk with God.

When the music began to play, people started to clap, praise, and shout to God! The enthusiastic praise I experienced as a young teenager! Revivals birthed a move of God, bringing back the lost and offering salvation to those who didn't know Jesus. As I stood to preach, I could feel the presence of God covering me from the crown of my head down to the soles of my feet. What a time we had the first night! Dad and Mom were so proud of me. Pleasing God and your parents bring a feeling that can't compare to anything else.

Thursday morning, we got up and had breakfast at the nearby IHOP. Dad began to feel sick a little nauseous. We stopped at a drugstore to get him some Alka-Seltzer and then went back to the hotel so he could rest. Once we were back in the hotel room, Dad laid down and drifted off to sleep. Later on, I decided it would be best for Mom to stay with Dad at the hotel while my cousin and I went to church. After church, Dad was still not feeling well. I was concerned, so early that Friday morning, we took my dad straight to the emergency room. The doctors there decided it would be best to admit him to the hospital.

I didn't want to leave Dad and Mom, but they assured me they would be okay there in the hospital. I hesitated, but I asked God to be with them until I returned.

I had an obligation to the church where I was conducting the revival, and completing that assignment was my parent's desire. My cousin and I prepared to drive back to the last night of the meeting. My parents were heavy on my mind, but I asked God to help me keep my thoughts together as I began to speak to His people. My subject that night was 'Lord Grow My Hair Back!' The word of the Lord compelled many to come to the altar, restoring them to the Father. The pastor was grateful to the Lord, and the congregation blessed. I breathed a big sigh of relief and thanked God for giving me the strength to complete the assignment.

I was anxious to return home; I picked up Mom and drove straight to the hospital! I didn't care if visiting hours were over. I needed to see my dad! I ran into the room and hugged him like it had been twenty days since I laid eyes on him. He asked, "Well, how did everything go. Did the church enjoy the revival?" Before I could answer his questions, he said, "I prayed for you, Shot!" That was almost too much for me to handle. I had never heard my dad say he prayed for me. I was sure he'd prayed for me before; he just never shared it with me. I saw how much my dad had grown in his walk with God that night.

Sadly, I saw my cousin off that following day. I thanked him for being such incredible support to me. He'd been with us all week, helping with Dad and giving me plenty of amens while I preached. I decided from that week on that he would be considered my brother. Being an only child can be lonely and leave you wishing you had a sibling. But he filled that void in me, and we've been inseparable ever since.

Mom and I headed back to the hospital Saturday morning. We met with the oncologist, and he wanted to run some tests on Dad. The tests would help pinpoint the problem so the doctor could treat the symptoms.

We sat in the waiting room for the doctor to explain the next step after he had gotten the test results. The doctor came out and gradually walked over to speak with us. He said he was upset with the surgeon who performed Dad's colon cancer surgery. He continued to tell us the surgeon had done a "sh*tty" job on my dad. He was so angry he wanted to fight the surgeon. I saw the disappointment in his eyes, and I felt his concern.

We thought he could solve the problem, and our lives would go back to normal. The following sentence out of the oncologist's mouth was, "I'm sorry. Mr. White has only six to nine months to live."

Mom began to scream, "Nooooooo, how can that be true?" The surgeon who performed the surgery said he removed all the colon cancer! The oncologist, moved by the emotion of the situation, held us both. I tried to console Mom and absorb her pain. I couldn't focus on my feelings, but the doctor helped us sit to gain our composure. We were stunned and paralyzed for quite some time. It felt like my life was on ten and had dropped to zero, quick, fast, and in a hurry.

How were we going to tell Dad and keep our faith intact? The doctor met with us in Dad's room to give him the test results. Mom and I stood on each side of the bed for strength and comfort. Dad heard the report and said, "I'll live out my days loving God and my family!" Oh my God! Dad shocked us, and we could only agree with his response. The doctor sent us home with prayers and apologies for the carelessness of his colleague who had performed the surgery.

I was thinking about what the oncologist told us, and it was troubling me. Did the surgeon help send a death sentence over my dad due to the terrible job of removing cancer in Dad's colon? How could he not do a good job and pretend he did? I was livid and couldn't believe what had just transpired. My dad could lose days, months, and possibly years of life due to another man's negligence.

Despite the news, we continued to live life to the fullest as a family. On the days that dad didn't feel well, we stayed with him at home. The dog understood that something was up too. Crystal, our Pekinese, would lay on the floor next to Dad when he didn't feel well. Dad did his best to hide his pain and emotions for Mom and me, and he didn't want us to see him in any discomfort.

In June, we traveled to Savanah to our family reunion. We suggested staying home, but Dad was determined to go. He was a man who dearly loved his family, and he didn't want to miss an opportunity to see them and tell them how much he loved them. Although he wasn't feeling his best and needed to lay down often, he was still going! I admired his strength, and it kept me inspired.

My aunt and uncle went along with us, and some of the other families from Waycross met us in Savanah. We were all happy to see each other. They were incredibly excited to see Dad after all he'd been through those past ten months. After seeing the joy on Dad's face as he hugged his family and told them how much he loved them, I was glad we had pressed to go. I couldn't help but wonder if this would be his last family reunion.

Chapter 3

Chapter 3
Daddy Leaves Me

The family gave those interested a chance to volunteer to host the next reunion. My dad raised his hand to our surprise. I didn't want to discourage him from hosting the family gathering. He loved his family so much, and I knew he was thinking of what an honor it would be to serve as their host. But I was greatly concerned about his health. I didn't want him to do anything that would drain his already dwindling strength. I was also thinking about the willingness of the other nearby relatives to come to help us with an event this large. I took a glance at my dad's face. He looked so focused, and how his hands clasped together told me there was no use in trying to convince him to let somebody else be the host. There would be no discussion! The family unanimously chose Dad to host the next White-Johnson-Ham Family Reunion.

Earlier, in 1997, Dad had suggested that the name of the gathering become 'The White Family Reunion.' He explained that we celebrated Austin and Hiram White and their descendants, and we added other persons as they married into the White family. 'The White Family Reunion' seemed significant to him. I had to admit that he was telling the truth and his argument was valid. While driving home from Savannah, Dad was noticeably excited about hosting the next reunion, and he talked about it almost all the way home. Even when he was quietly resting in the car's back seat, you could see the wheels of his mind turning. He had big plans.

As July approached, Dad's health began to decline noticeably. He was experiencing more stomach pain, and he was eating less. At that point, every vision I'd had from the Lord was ever before me. I couldn't shake the visuals any longer. Even discussing it with Mom didn't feel like it was the right thing to do. I wanted to keep her from as much emotional pain as possible. There were days that I would stop at my house after work before seeing my parents. I'd cry my eyes out, praying for my strength, mercy, and healing for Dad. I tried not to break down and lose it before my parents became an everyday chore.

Mom sold out to the idea of saving her beloved husband's life at any cost. Someone suggested we try alternative medicine for my Dad. Mom, Dad, and I agreed that this was an option. We made an appointment and flew, with Dad's medical records, speaking with the doctors who were practicing the then-popular alternative methods of treating cancer. They performed a procedure that they believed would extend my dad's life. We thought we were doing what was in my dad's best interest. We arrived back home with new hope.

It felt good to be home, taking care of Dad. We kept a close eye on him, watching for any signs of improvement, continuously believing for the best. One night, he began to toss and turn, moaning in such excruciating pain, that we quickly dressed and took him to the emergency room. Mom, dad's sister, and I waited anxiously in the seated area. Our nerves had kept us on edge while we waited. The comfort of the Holy Spirit warmed us and brought strength as we waited. Finally, the doctor came out and explained what we already knew. He recommended we prepare to make the rest of Dad's time with us as comfortable as possible. Those were difficult words to swallow, and the mental pain I experienced was indescribable.

We knew Dad's condition was severe, but we didn't expect the news we received from the emergency room doctor. The weight of our reality and fear suddenly became overwhelming. The three of us began to cry out to God, asking Him to help us, show mercy, and give us just a little more time with my Dad. Many of those sitting in the waiting room looked at us with empathy as we processed what we'd just heard. Their compassion showed in their eyes, and they became silent out of respect for our apparent sorrow.

The doctors prescribed Dad pain meds, and we prepared to take him home. Once again, I called relatives and friends, updating them on Dad's health. I was grateful to God for people in my life who were concerned about my family. One friend, in particular, began to come over daily after work to sit with us and help us take care of Dad. Some nights I needed to leave my parent's house early to release my emotions. I had come to terms with God's decision to take my father home to be with Him. My friend would let me cry without encouraging me to hide the depth of my sadness. Sometimes, when you are a minister of the gospel, people believe that nothing should, or does, rattle you.

The doctor ordered a hospital bed for Dad to be more comfortable lying down. At that point, his mobility had become little to none, and oxygen helped his lungs breathe. The hum and the hiss of the machine were a constant reminder of the degree of difficulty he had taking a breath. We refused hospice services because the thought of having to watch Dad take his last breath at home was too much for Mom and me. We understood that we would be forfeiting the right to resuscitate my dad when that time came. Dad had begun talking about visions of his grandmother. We knew his days on earth were coming to an end. Mom and I still hadn't discussed his death, believing, and hoping God would eventually heal him.

While our lives were already in chaos, the last thing we needed was the threat of a hurricane. Tropical storms and hurricanes usually wreaked havoc during September month. Hurricane Floyd, which was forecasted to be a category five storm, was heading straight to the east and likely directly hitting our coast. We struggled to find a safe place for Dad to weather the enormous potential of the superstorm. The hospitals refused to admit him because they considered him a terminally ill patient. What a blow! Their thought process is that he is dying, so we will accommodate those not terminally ill.

While trying to keep Mom calm, I prayed to God that He would turn the storm and not allow it to hit our area. The National Weather Service predicted that Floyd would possibly be the most devastating storm ever to hit our coast. Massive flooding, gale-force winds, and downed power lines were inevitable.

That night, we plugged in our weather radio to keep informed about the storm's proximity. I've learned that we should never stop praying for God's mercy, even it appears that He won't be answering the way we hope He will. So, I continued to pray.

Dad insisted that we bring the weather radio in the bedroom so he could hear what was going on as well. As the announcer gave the tracking miles for the storm, Dad told jokes and talked about everything that came to his mind. The more disturbing and frightening the weather report got, the more Dad talked and told jokes. He kept asking for fruit and crackers to eat. I thought that was weird because, up to that point, Dad's appetite had been bird-like, at best. But, deep down, Dad knew we were frightened and worried about his safety. He wanted to direct our attention away from the hurricane. I believe he prayed to keep us all safe from the storm, knowing we were doing everything we could to take care of him.

God answered our prayers, and hurricane Floyd made an unexpected turn before making landfall. As the announcer on the weather radio gave us the all-clear, we all raised our hands and shouted, "Thank you, Jesus!" Even our dog, which had just been trying to stay out the way, began jumping up and down. I guess she thought she should be doing what we were doing. The relief and the humor of that moment will always be a reminder of how much God cares.

About a week later, Dad went to the emergency room again. This time the doctor said his blood pressure was continuing to drop; he was dying. Well, I wasn't ready to let go of Dad, and neither was my mom. We began to pray and ask God for his life. Forty minutes passed, and the doctor came out to see us. He looked somewhat astonished as he approached us in the waiting room. He said, "I don't know what has happened, but Mr. White's blood pressure is normal, and he's telling jokes!" The doctor didn't understand, but we knew God had made the difference. After admitting Dad to the cancer floor, we waited patiently to see him. He asked if we were okay, we answered all was well!

A couple of days later, while visiting Dad after work, he asked, "Shot, when is Jesus coming to get me?" His question caught me off guard. For the first time, I realized that Dad was probably tired of being in pain, tired of the exhausting trips back and forth to the emergency room. He was ready to see Jesus. The Man that saved him from his sins.

Tears began to well up in my eyes, and before I knew it, they began to flow down my face. As steadily as I could, I managed to say, "If you are ready, He will come for you." My heart was overwhelmingly sorrowful, but I was happy that Dad knew his soul was right with God, and he understood that he was waiting on God. I knew that I needed to release him and let him peacefully go to the Father with resistance in my heart.

I met my mom and aunt in the hospital cafeteria a few minutes later. I decided it was time to share all my visions from the Lord I'd had over the last year and a half. It was painful telling them we needed to let go so Dad could return to the Father. Our prayers kept him alive for our comfort, but he was ready to go. We began to pray for the strength to surrender our will over to the Sovereignty of God.

Dad and his first cousins grew up together like siblings. The bond they shared was incredible. Everyone was praying and concerned. One evening we received a call from Aunt Sister, who lived in Georgia, as we affectionately called one of his first cousins. Without me asking, Aunt Sister had planned to come and stay with us until Dad went home to be with Jesus. She explained that she wanted to be with Dad,

Mom, and myself; she just wanted to be supportive during this challenging time. Boy, did I appreciate that! Mom would arrive at the hospital religiously every morning by 10 a.m. and stay until Dad's lunch tray was served and collected. After that, she would go home to rest for a couple of hours, then return to the hospital at 6 p.m. I didn't want her to be at home alone for those couple of hours. I knew she wasn't getting the proper rest; she couldn't relax. Without asking God, He fulfilled my heart's desire. He sent my aunt from Georgia to help fill those restless hours my mom spent at home.

Mom shared with me that the doctors medicated Dad heavily to ease the pain and discomfort of the disease that had taken over his body. Dad wasn't talking as much, and Mom attributed that to the powerful medicines pumping into his veins. The following Saturday, I drove Mom and Aunt to visit Dad in the hospital. While they were gone to the cafeteria for lunch, I settled into the chair beside Dad's bed.

Suddenly, he called my name! "Shot, come over here," he said. I was shocked and didn't know how to react because I thought he couldn't speak! The expression on my face was probably worth a thousand words. I got up from the chair beside his bed, leaned in close, and said, "Daddy, I thought you couldn't speak!"

His response was one of the most selfless answers ever expressed from a dying man. He said, "I love your momma very much. I know I will leave her, so I want to prepare her for our separation. When she comes to see me, I look at her and turn my back to her so that she won't see my tears." I began to cry, and I hugged him, never wanting to let go. If I

63

didn't realize my dad's love for Mom, the moment of truth was here.

That day he gave me specific instructions on how to take care of Mom for him. I couldn't stop crying; for the first time, I knew that I wasn't going to have my hero available. Mom had always told me that, as a child, I would cry to follow him. Sometimes, he would take me along with him, and other times he would bring me candy to cheer me up after he left me. He taught me how to fish and hunt, and whatever I saw him eating, I was willing to try. Whenever I thought Mom would say no, I would ask Dad, knowing that his answer would always be 'yes.' Two peas in a pod explained our relationship. Dad taught great lessons, and I'll never forget them. The thought of him leaving my life was more than I could manage.

Word traveled that Dad was rapidly declining. His fishing buddies, hunting buddies, and partying buddies began to visit him. Many of them hadn't seen him in years, but they wanted to see him for one last time. My strength felt as though it was failing me emotionally. Thank God my friend continued to be supportive as my family hung on to Dad's life. There were nights I stayed at my parent's home until 11 p.m., and even on those long nights, my friend was there, knowing how much my heart was bleeding.

There were so many visitors; we often left the room to let them have special moments alone with Dad. Little did we know that he was giving our family and friends instructions on how to take care of his family. He realized that he covered so many areas in our lives, and his death would leave a huge hole, and it would be an adjustment for us. As his friends left the house, we would greet them again, thanking them for their time and consideration for Dad.

We consoled many of them as they cried and shared their experiences with him. I began to hear how much of a leader Dad was among his peers. Some even shared how he called and gave them food to last for a couple of days, not knowing that they had no food except for what he brought. There were things shared about how he inspired the young boys on our street to become hunters and taught them how to cook the wildlife they hunted well. I watched on many occasions; Dad gave money to help others when they didn't have enough to meet their needs. He was not a perfect man, but he was a caring man.

I requested personal leave from my job to be by my dad's side and support my mom and aunt. I often sat near his bed, holding his hand, reflecting on moments from my childhood, which helped me praise God in my sadness. I wanted him to know I was there with him through this unknown journey. I wanted him to hear my voice as I whispered how proud I was of him and that it was okay for him to leave Mom and me. I no longer wanted him to be in unbearable pain for my benefit.

Dad's primary doctor came for a visit and said they were releasing my dad from the hospital; there wasn't anything else they could do for him. I was stunned by the doctor's lack of empathy and cold demeanor. Why would they send a man home with only a couple of days to live? We couldn't take care of his needs! We had no idea what to do.

Later that day, a nurse came in with some paperwork to be confirmed. Someone had signed a Do Not Resuscitate order, and it was clear that the primary doctor had decided my dad's fate without consulting us and without getting our permission. We had never authorized any forms that would give the hospital the right to do a DNR on my dad at any time. We were livid and demanded to see the signature on the form and made sure they knew that we had also summoned legal assistance. The hospital immediately shredded the falsified documents before us, and we received new paperwork that correctly stated our wishes for my dad's care.

Mom had already expressed that she didn't want Dad to die at home. I began to petition God for a way that he could remain hospitalized until his death. Within a couple of hours, a new doctor I hadn't met before came to speak with us. He identified himself as the doctor in charge of my dad's discharge orders. Mom and I approached him with significant concerns. He looked at Dad's chart and said, "Mr. White has a fever, and I've decided against discharging him." He winked at us as if God Himself had sent him on assignment to answer our prayers. I believed we encountered an angel sent by God to stop the plans of an uncaring doctor. God still showed us how much He loved us and cared about our circumstances and pain.

By this time, Dad could no longer verbally communicate with us. I began to feel like his time here on earth was coming to an end soon. I was grateful to my aunt for spending three weeks with us. I left the room sometimes because I couldn't digest the moment. Going and not feeling guilty for leaving Mom alone was a relief. I felt like I couldn't deal with my pain because I knew Mom struggled in a way I couldn't understand. I just wanted to be there for her in any shape or form that she needed.

Another one of my aunts called on the following Friday night, letting us know they were coming to visit Dad and be with us for the weekend. I tried to talk them out of traveling, but I was thankful for the additional support inside. They decided to dismiss my advice, and they arrived early that Saturday morning. We got up early that morning to prepare to go to the hospital to meet them. Just as I opened the door to leave for the hospital, the phone rang. The Caller's I.D. display showed the call was coming from the hospital. I was afraid to answer, and my hands began to sweat. I managed to pick up the receiver and say hello. The voice on the other end confirmed the words I had been dreading for so long; "Mr. White is passing," and we thought you would want to be with him during his transition.

I thought I couldn't cry anymore, but the tears ran like a faucet as I hurriedly got Mom and my aunt in the car. I drove to the hospital as if I was in a drag race. I put on my hazard lights, hoping everyone would understand that I was in a hurry and just get out of my way!

We arrived at the hospital, and I put Mom in a wheelchair for quicker mobility. My aunt and uncle met the three of us at the door of Dad's room. They had been there thirty minutes before we arrived. They hugged us, and we all cried together. I was so glad they had a chance to see Dad before he passed away. Moving frantically, I called Dad's brothers to come and be with us during Dad's transition. The nurse told us that he would probably live for another thirty minutes to an hour. It seemed that my dad's siblings drove a rocket to get to the hospital; within minutes, they were there in the room with us.

I took Mom over to Dad's bedside to be with him. The nurses had already unhooked all the tubes, and Dad laid there motionless while taking slow, shallow breaths. Mom began to tell him how much she loved him and that she was proud of him for accepting Jesus into his heart. Mom also expressed how he had been an excellent provider and a great father to me. Lastly, she told him, "Shot and I will be okay, so don't worry. God has us in His arms."

After sharing her sentiments, speaking from the place of a committed wife, she nodded for me to come and share my heart. The emotions I felt were unexplainable. Trying to process that our time together left was only a few minutes was unimaginable. Although God had been preparing me for His Sovereign Will, it still hurt deeply to let go of him.

The nurses came by frequently to check on Dad, showering us with sympathy and compassion. They had many moments where their patients succumbed to their illnesses. But they never made us feel like this was an ordinary occurrence, and I watched them check his heart and pulse, and I could tell by the look on their faces that death was at the door.

As I sat staring at Dad, I began to tell him how much I loved him again and how I was proud to be his daughter. Vivid memories flashed through my mind, and my tears overflowed like a river breaking through a dam. I thought about how my dad was an entrepreneur cleaning, cooking, and selling wildlife. During the hunting season, dad and his good friend would catch a lot of coons (aka) raccoons. He would clean them, bag them up, and place them in a cooler on ice. The fun would begin as we visited the hangouts where men played cards and dominos. Dad drove up, honking his horn like the ice cream man! The men would drop what they were doing to come and buy a 'coon from Clint. I watched and paid attention to detail. The conversations always started when the buyer saw the size of the 'coon before the price of the 'coon. Dad would lay the 'coons down with the price hidden. He wanted the buyer to fall in love with the size before they saw the price; what a genius, I must say! Once the buyer saw the price sometimes, they would say twenty-five dollars is too much to pay for a 'coon. Then Daddy would say, well, I have some neckbone' coons right here which were smaller and priced at fifteen dollars. The buyer usually ended up buying a twenty-dollar 'coon. Dad and I would burst out with laughter after the buyers left! Where did he get that concept? Who would know that I would become an entrepreneur like my amazing Dad later in life?

Mom was so sweet, and she was doing her best to be strong for me. She came over and dried my tears and hugged me while she prayed over me. Her prayers began to soothe the unbearable pain I was experiencing. She knew that even in times of sorrow, her God was still her rock, and He'd never leave us.

In the last four days, Dad's strength was utterly exhausted. He lost his ability to blink and move other parts of his body. So, I knew he could only hear what we were saying. Then a surprising thing happened! Suddenly, Dad opened his eyes and looked straight at me. He miraculously gained enough strength to rise from his pillow, pointing upward towards the heavens. Dad threw the blanket off the upper portion of his body. I looked at his mouth, and he was moving his lips, trying to tell me something. He kept looking at me and then looking upward while pointing. I began to look up towards the ceiling. I never saw any images, but I

69

heard chariots, and it was coming from the heavens. I could not believe what my ears were hearing. Dad saw the angels coming for him to take him home. He was trying to show me what he saw in the spirit realm. What a glorious vision it was for him. Dad went through those motions for about three minutes, and then he gradually slowed down and took his last breath.

I screamed, feeling a pain I had never experienced, "Jesus! Dad is gone!" Watching him take his last breath, pointing towards heaven, is a bittersweet memory for me. Immediately the room filled with moans and outcries from Mom and all his siblings. They tried to console each other as much as possible. There is only so much you can do to prepare for death. I took his arms, placed them by his side, and pulled the cover to his chest while looking as if he were peacefully sleeping. Mom slowly approached his bed, reaching out to hold his hand. Her tears covered his face, and she sobbed as if she was heartbroken.

I went to the nurse's station to inform them of Dad's passing, and the nurse offered condolences and came to the room to officially pronounce him deceased. Everyone had left except me, Mom, and two of my aunts. We were not ready to go, and we would go back and forth and stare at Dad's lifeless body and rub his head.

After about forty-five minutes, the oncology doctor greeted everyone, identifying himself. He then turned to Dad and said, "Hello, Mr. White. How are you feeling?" We were looking at each other, utterly confused by the doctor's actions. Did he not know that Dad was dead?

I began to say to myself, Jesus, if you are getting ready to wake up my dad, I need a heads up! Because if he answers the doctor, I don't know if we'll be here for the conversation! The doctor went over to the bed and gently tried to wake Dad. Finally, I could not hold back the laughter! "I'm sorry, Doc, but Mr. White died forty-five minutes ago." By this time, Mom and my aunts were laughing hysterically. The doctor began to apologize over and over while turning beet red. He was embarrassed and angry with the nurse's station. They had never updated Dad's chart to include that he had expired. We assured him that everything was all right. We needed that laugh to break up that moment of pain.

Chapter 4

Chapter 4

A Daughter's Love For Her Daddy

The nurses were very kind to us, knowing it was hard to leave Dad. We were still in a state of shock, feeling paralyzed, not able to walk away. I had decided that I would take Mom home whenever she decided she was ready to go. There was still a hint of Dad's warmth in the room, and I understood how difficult it was to leave that warmth. It would be like removing the comfort of a warm blanket to be exposed to the chill of a cold night. We would stay as long as there was the slightest degree of warmth there.

Eventually, Mom stood up, walked to Dad's bedside, kissed his silent lips, and gently rubbed his head. Death had finally separated a relationship that started when they were just fourteen years old. I remember Mom telling me how Dad would walk her halfway home from school and then return to football practice. She always told that story with the same giggly lovesick enthusiasm of a teenage girl. Her face always showed that she was reliving the giddiness that comes with young love. So, it hurt me painfully to watch her trying to prepare to move on in life without her beloved husband of thirty-six years.

After spending that brief private moment with him, Mom called my two aunts and me to come and share that moment with her. We each spoke our hearts through the tears, gathered our things, and slowly walked to the nurse's station. The nurses once again offered condolences, and we extended our thanks.

The slow walk to the car was long and painful. The ride from the hospital was even longer, and it seemed like the longest ride of my life. If you could have heard our tears falling onto the front of our clothing, that would have been the only noise. The drive was silent as we were all trying to find our way to adjust to the will of God. Dad was never coming home again, and we would never hear him laugh again, never smell his cologne as he dressed for church again, never see his praise, and never enjoy his great cooking again.

We arrived at the house, hearing the phone ringing before unlocking the door. Within an hour, family, friends, neighbors, and church members flowed through the front door. They sat with us, doing whatever they could to console us. They brought tons of food and gallons of southern sweetened drinks. We were overwhelmed by the love and concern shown to us in the passing of the man we all loved so dearly. Dad had not always known Jesus during his lifetime, but he had always had the heart to help people. So, even the unsaved wanted to share how much he had impacted their lives. Everybody had a story to tell, and I wanted to hear them all.

Finally, I convinced Mom to go to bed to rest her mind and body. I stayed up and greeted those who kept filing in the door. Dad's death was a tremendous shock for many, and I was somewhat surprised to know how many people were touched by his heart to help. It was almost 10 p.m. when the last visitor left to go home. I was emotionally exhausted and physically drained of strength. I had spent the entire day helping others deal with the grief associated with my dad's death, and I hadn't even taken the time to process my feelings of loss. I think God had it planned that way so that I could hear others speak about the positive attributes of my dad. Every story blessed me and strengthened my heart, but just the knowledge and the assurance that Dad had accepted Christ brought me the most comfort.

I got up early and made breakfast for Mom and my aunt the next day. We sat at the dining room table, reminiscing about Dad and his comedic personality. Oh, the stories we told and heard were enough to provide material for a complete stage show. One of my favorite stories was about the hunting dog named Cindy and the tiger 'coon (aka) raccoon.

Dad and his good buddy would go hunting every Saturday morning for a couple of months out of the year. His buddy introduced him to his new hunting dog sensation, Cindy, a pit bull. Her reputation for fighting and killing her opponent made her a force to be reckoned with! One morning before one of those legendary hunting trips, my dad said to his buddy, "Man, I don't know if Cindy can handle a 'coon." Dad had been hunting for enough years to know that raccoons could put up a ferocious fight, and they never gave up quickly. But there was no changing his buddy's mind. He was convinced that Cindy would fight the 'coons, killing them with no problem. Dad admitted that Cindy was a big pit, strong, with broad shoulders, and he would give her a try.

The following morning came, and Dad loaded up his bluetick-hounds and headed to his buddy's house. There, they loaded the cage for the dogs, placing Cindy in the cage with the hounds. She was pretty big compared to the other hunting dogs, but Dad still wasn't entirely convinced that she could handle a 'coon hunt. His buddy reassured him that Cindy would make them proud, or at least he thought.

As the sun crept over the horizon, they arrived at their hunting spot. The hounds were excited, and as soon as the men opened the cage doors, all the bluetick hounds jumped out of the cage and took off. Cindy hesitated, slowly jumping out of the cage, standing beside her master and saying, 'what do I do now?' According to my dad, that was the first sign that maybe bringing Cindy along wasn't such a good idea.

The hunters followed the sounds of barking deep into the woods. Cindy trotted beside my dad's buddy as if they were out for a morning jog. When they got close to the barking, they became excited as the hounds indicated that they had found a raccoon. They followed the sounds to the bank of a small river. The 'coon was in a tree, just looking down at them as the hounds frantically barked up at it.

When Dad began to shoot at the 'coon, it jumped into the water to escape. They then realized it was no ordinary thirteen-pound 'coon, but a huge forty-five-pound tiger 'coon. It had stripes on its ears and a tail like a tiger. The tiger 'coons were fierce and aggressive fighters. Its size alone increased the chance of injuring one of the hounds. The hounds were ready to jump in and fight the 'coon. But nooooooo, Dad's hunting partner threw Cindy in the water. Instinctively, Cindy began to swim toward the 'coon with lightning speed. Eager for a fight, she was growling and baring a full set of angry teeth. As soon as she got close, the tiger 'coon reached out and slapped Cindy. Cindy shook off the attack and pounced on top of the tiger 'coon. My dad's buddy yelled, "There you go, Cindy! You got 'em!"

Daddy waded out into the water to get a better angle to shoot the 'coon. After a while, they heard a lot of flapping and slapping on the water. The tiger 'coon was on top of Cindy's head, drowning her. Dad's partner began screaming from the riverbank. He jumped up and down, shouting, "We're going to have to rescue Cindy!"

Since Dad was closer to the brawling animals, he quickly ran toward them. Every time he said that story, he swore he heard Cindy say, "Shooooooot him!" Dad ended up hitting the 'coon with the butt of his shotgun to save Cindy's life. Then he shot and killed the prize. Cindy was too tired to swim back to shore, so Dad dragged her out of the water and laid her at her master's feet. He then returned to the water to retrieve the tiger 'coon. Cindy was altogether out of breath for fifteen minutes laying on the bank with her tongue hung out as she gasped for air. My dad's buddy knelt beside her and tried to comfort her by patting her belly. When she finally recovered enough to make it back to the truck, they put her in the cage, where she stayed until the day of hunting was over.

The dogs rode home in the cage. The raccoons they caught were placed on top of the cage. Cindy still hadn't completely recovered from the trauma of almost being drowned by the tiger 'coon. She laid in the far corner of the cage, away from the loud barking hounds. When my dad's truck hit a bump in the road, one of the 'coon's tails fell through the opening on top of the cage. Unfortunately, the tail hit Cindy. She went crazy! She started fighting and biting the hound dogs as if she had completely lost her mind. Dad yelled for his buddy to pull the truck over and get Cindy out of the cage before she hurt one of the other dogs. They somehow managed to get the enraged pit bull out of the cage, and she quietly rode in the truck's front seat all the way home.

The following Saturday morning, as they were getting ready to go hunting, they put the blue-tick hounds in the cage. Dad said that when they looked over at Cindy, she growled and rolled her eyes at them. That day, Cindy was officially retired as a 'coon dog. From that day on, she just watched the house.

As I retold that story the morning after Dad passed, we laughed so hard, we cried. Dad could tell you a lie and persuade you to believe it because he was such a good storyteller. I was on a roll, so I refilled everybody's coffee cup and shared more stories.

During Dad's partying days, I could get him to come with us to church when Mom couldn't. We had an evangelist from down south running a tent revival at one point, and word went out about the miracles and good singing going on under the tent. Excited, I wanted to go and see for myself, and I wanted Dad to come with us.

The tent had been in town for about three weeks when I finally asked Dad to go. He agreed to join me, and we planned a night to go. As soon as we drove up, we could hear the praises and the great music. Mom, Dad, my aunt, and I went in and sat together. The evangelist's wife played the organ, and his children played the drums. He believed in the laying on of hands while praying for the attendees. In each service, he would call for those who wanted prayer. The Lord used him to bring many to Christ and deliver people from drugs and prostitution, and other problems.

Dad could find something funny in any situation. Church services were no exception. The first thing that happened while enjoying the revival service was that a lady went up for prayer, and the evangelist accidentally knocked her wig off her head. Dad and I laughed like we were at home in the kitchen! The more we tried to pull ourselves together, the more we laughed. Mom looked down the row at us and gave us the 'stank-face,' but it only worsened. The spirit was high, and everyone was shouting and giving God praise. Thank goodness the music and the voices of the worshippers covered our giggles and snorts. By the time things got quiet, Dad and I had given in to the exhaustion of hideous laughter. Mom was just left shaking her head.

Again, the spirit rose, and the audience broke into high praise and worship. Suddenly, my dad hunched me in my side and discreetly nodded toward his left shoulder. I followed his gaze and saw that over to the left of the tent; a large hippy lady had grabbed hold of one of the poles used to hold up the tent. She began to shake her hips while she was praising God. Dad leaned over to me and whispered, "Wait a minute! Is that who I think it is?" The worshipping lady was shaking like a woman he'd seen many times in the club. Sure enough, it turned out that she was the same woman who used to hold the jukebox in the club and gyrate her enormous hips!

After church, Dad couldn't wait to put on a show! He had collected so much new material that night. He grabbed the kitchen bar, imitating the lady holding the pole, swinging his little manly hips from side to side. At first, Mom pretended she disapproved of his little show. Eventually, everybody was laughing. We screamed and laughed until our sides hurt, and tears were streaming down our cheeks. I rolled all over the couch, begging him to stop. Who would have thought you'd see twerking at a revival service! We laughed and cried until we couldn't do anything else. Dad's visual was too much, and I didn't know if I would ever be able to go back to that tent without visualizing my dad shaking his itty-bitty hips. And I didn't know if I could compose myself if I were there, and that lady grabbed that pole and started shaking her hips while praising God. Lord, I would need help!

Although signs, wonders, and miracles were happening every night, everyone didn't approve of the tent services. There was a lot of controversy over church members from various denominations attending these services. Some local pastors were angry and demanded that their members stop visiting the services or face disciplinary action for their participation. My aunt and a few other members continued going despite the warnings. As a result, they were disciplined and could no longer be a part of any auxiliaries in their church.

Needless to say, that whole disciplinary action thing didn't sit well with my Dad. He just couldn't believe that his sister received punishment for enjoying the benefits of attending the tent revival. He had some pretty choice words for the whole situation, and it bothered him that the local pastors had a problem with the 'any way You bless me, Lord' atmosphere of the tent revivals. He didn't understand how the pastors could begrudge the participants of their blessings under the tent.

One participant was in the final stages of terminal cancer. The tent evangelist prayed for her, and her cancer went into remission. Threatened by her leadership, she stopped attending the revival. A few months later, the Lord visited me concerning her. Her daughter, who brought her to the tent revival, was also part of the vision.

In the vision, all three of us were crossing a river together. The water was calm and just waist-deep. Suddenly, the lady who had cancer said she was too tired to go any further. Her daughter and I tried to encourage her just to keep going. We pointed out that she was only a few feet away from the other side, but we could not convince her that she could make it if she had just kept moving forward. Shortly after that vision, one of the church members told me that my friend's Mother's cancer was no longer in remission. My heart was sad for her because I knew she would die. Just as I thought, she died within a couple of months after that vision. When I explained everything to my Dad, he shook his head and pointed out that she may have lived if she had continued attending the tent revivals.

Eventually, his anger gave way to humor, and he teased us about how we were going to 'get it' for sneaking off to the revivals. Dad had a way of pointing out the humor in even the most difficult situations. I loved that about him, and I knew I would miss his lighthearted approach to life.

The following Monday, we started handling the necessary preparation to bury my dad. Mom held up through her tears, and I told her it was alright to cry, and she didn't have to hide her sorrow for my sake. So, I held her hand while we talked to the mortician and made the final arrangements. That seemed to help her just as much as it helped me.

We also completed a great deal of the business that day. Dad had made some arrangements for our financial security. The financial institution that held the lien on their vehicle informed Mom that Dad had taken out a policy that would pay the car off in the event of his death. As soon as Mom heard about all the thoughtful preparations Dad had made, she began to bawl and praise God. She turned to me and said, "Your father lived for the future."

Mom was correct about Dad believing you shouldn't live only for the moment. I had many precious memories of my dad. He loved me unconditionally during my time of trying to run from my pain and living life outside of God. I remember when I returned home to the Lord from a life of carelessness. Dad did what God did for me spiritually in the natural. Just as God had wiped away my sins through repentance, cleansing me by the blood He shed on Calvary; Dad paid the debts I incurred while I was irresponsibly using credit cards to pay for nights spent in hotels. He said, "Shot, I want you to have a fresh start and not worry about your mistakes." He could have allowed me to struggle financially to teach me a lesson, but because he loved me and only wanted the very best for me. God could have let me not flourish spiritually to teach me a lesson. But because He loves me and wants what is best for me, He completely forgave me and restored my spiritual standing. I was undoubtedly blessed.

There were so many things that needed to be taken care of for my dad's funeral. The arrangements, gathering clothes the morticians would put on Dad's body for the funeral, and program participants had to be contacted and confirmed to print the program. I dreaded the trip to the funeral home, but I knew it was necessary, and I knew it would be traumatic and more painful than anything we could handle alone emotionally. Before we left for the funeral home, I took a few minutes to walk next door to my house to kneel and pray. I asked God, "Please be with us and give us the strength to have this meeting in preparation to bury my daddy. We don't have the strength or the stamina to keep it together, God."

Just like an anchor, God kept us steady. He didn't let us down. He provided us with the strength and the clarity of thought we needed to choose a casket and arrange Daddy's funeral. We were blessed to know people who worked professionally in the funeral business. Our cousin's boyfriend arrived that Wednesday to write the obituary and type the final copy of the program. My cousin, who I had chosen as my brother, also drove down the same day to support us. We were so thankful for everyone who showed us so much love during that challenging time. Our hearts were encouraged. Things were falling into place.

Praise Fellowship Community Choir officers offered to minister in song for the funeral. I hadn't been worried about the music or the eulogist, but it was nice to have those things already prepared. The choir scheduled a rehearsal, and I decided only to sing uplifting songs for the funeral. Along with allowing us to use their facility for the funeral, the host church also provided ushers for the service. The other church members and friends worked out the details for the repast that was to take place after the burial. The to-do list was gradually getting shorter.

The funeral home asked us to bring Dad's funeral garments Thursday morning. I had already discussed with my mom the past vision I had of Dad in a brown casket, dressed in a brown suit. Honoring Dad, we all dressed in matching attire as a family for the last time. Mom wore a crisp beige suit and hat, and I wore an identical brown suit.

Even choosing our clothing was emotional, and we knew this was the last time we could publicly honor Dad together.

That Friday came quickly, and Dad's body was ready for family viewing. We checked every detail, making sure he looked his absolute best. Mom and I purchased the brown suit worn on Father's Day the previous year. Never in a million years did I think he would only get to wear it a couple of times before we would bury him in it. He liked how he looked in a suit and wore them on special occasions and whenever he went to church. He even enjoyed shopping for them. He didn't mind trying on different suits until he found the right color and fit. He would say, "Shot, let's go to the Men's store, and I want you to pick out a nice suit, tie, and shirt for Daddy!" I loved those trips to the Men's store, coordinating his clothes for him. I wanted him always to be sporty, clean, and smelling good when he left home. He was dressed for the last time now, and I still wanted him to look good.

I knew this was another challenging moment for our family. Seeing Dad lying there lifeless, not being able to smile, talk, or hug us was traumatizing. All week I tried to visualize how Mom would hold up through it all. Family and friends continued to shower us with love and affection, but occasionally I left the crowds to pray for strength and sanity. I knew I needed to be strong so Mom would feel comfortable leaning on me.

Slowly my family and I walked into the funeral home. Although we had just entered, we could see Dad's profile from the doorway. Mom screamed as I had never heard before. It was clear that the emotional pain was more than we could measure. My cousin and I held her arms as she stumbled forward, and we tightened our grip on her to keep her from falling. Tears were streaming down my face, and my heart was aching, but my primary concern was for my mom. Immediately, my tongues of intercession began to intercede for us all. It was clear that we were all visibly shaken. The Holy Spirit did his excellent work, and we were immediately comforted.

Mom made her way forward to the side of Dad's casket. She began to straighten Dad's necktie and gently smooth down his mustache. She had known and loved him for forty-five years, and they were married for thirty-six years. She certainly knew when Dad looked his best. Cancer and radiation treatments had taken a toll on Dad's appearance, and his weight loss and skin discoloration were evident. Even with those factors, the funeral directors made Dad look well and peaceful. We were pleased, considering the trauma he experienced.

After seating Mom, it was my turn to stand over my father. While my cousin walked with me up to the casket, my knees began to buckle. The reality was setting in that my dad was no longer here in the flesh, and I would never hear him call me 'Shot' again. A voice said, *"Your God wasn't faithful, and he let your daddy die despite your prayers."* The voice spoke clearly and loudly, as if it was coming from a speaker sitting on my shoulder.

I knew I had to come back with something more excellent. I couldn't let the devil have the final say. I began to repeat softly, *"God loves me, and He saved my daddy from eternal hell!"* I admit I was crushed and saddened by his death, but I refused to believe God was negligent.

I started patting Daddy's head, gently touching his face and smoothing his tie. I went through those motions for a few minutes, and I couldn't step away from him. "Daddy, I love you, and I'm going to take care of Mom." Those seemed to be the only words my lips could form. I laid my head on his chest one last time. I knew nothing I could say or do would change that he wasn't coming back.

My aunts and uncles were a total mess too! Dad influenced them with his actions and his love for his entire family. He kept our family together after my great aunt passed away in many ways. It hurt me to see my aunts and uncles struggling to cope with their brother's death. They needed much prayer and consoling, too. We finally informed the funeral home staff that we were ready to leave. We thanked them for working to achieve Dad's natural look. We endured another quiet ride back to the house.

We scheduled the public viewing for later that day at 5 p.m. I tried to convince Mom to stay at home and continue to rest. She said, "No, I'm going to be alright." She made a deal with me, though. She promised me that she would only stay for an hour. She needed to have a final glimpse of Dad, and I understood that. I knew how difficult it was for me to leave him, so I know it had to have been even more difficult for Mom. We decided that we would not view the body during the funeral. The trauma of re-opening the casket at the funeral would delay our ability to start the closure process. Mom did well through her tears. She spent her hour greeting people and helping them deal with their grief.

I kept an eye on the time, ensuring Mom didn't stay longer than our previously agreed-upon hour. My aunts drove a different vehicle, and I was relieved that Mom kept her word and went home with them as her hour extended stay was over. Family and friends came to pay their last respects to Dad. I knew some of them, and others told me stories of how they knew Mr. White. The stories were amazing and funny. Dad had more of an impact on people than I imagined. As the time began to wind down, I could feel a level of anxiety trying to creep its way into my spirit.

As the visitation time ended, anxiety aggressively invaded my peace. After I left Dad this time, I knew that I would never see him again on the earth, and I hesitated and started wishing for more time to be there with him. Everyone had left, and I stood by the casket, quietly sobbing. My brother hugged me, reminded me how much my dad loved me, and reassured me that he was proud of me. We turned and walked away, and that was the last time I saw my daddy.

The president of the High School class of 1958 Alumni Association called to let us know they would be traveling early that Saturday morning to be present at the funeral. Over the years, Dad had faithfully attended his class reunions, and his classmates wanted to make sure they were there to say goodbye to him. Many other relatives and friends from Georgia also came to honor Dad's life. We extended an invitation to all of them to view Dad's body the hour before the funeral started. The casket would be closed as we processed into the church.

When we arrived at the church, we were shocked by the number of cars in the parking lot. As we walked up the stairs to the church, we saw the church filled. It blessed Mom and me to see so many people in attendance.

At 11 a.m., the processional began its slow march down the church's center aisle to the sound of great music and praise. The choir sang my dad's favorite song, "Just Can't Stop Praising His Name!" Watching him dance and praise God while we worshipped had always been a joy. I imagined him saying, 'Shot, they're playing my song!' Holding Mom's hand, we walked at her pace to our seats at the very front of the church. Through the tears, we praised God, and we felt His presence comforting us.

Dad would have approved his program. He had always stressed that he didn't want any 'asas' meaning as a friend, neighbor, or coworker. We always laughed when he said that, not realizing that one day we were going to have the chance to follow through with his humorous request. He would have been pleased to see that we had honored his directions.

The presence of God met us in our darkest hour. You could feel it in the atmosphere. Most of the people in attendance knew Dad when he didn't know Christ. The last five years of his life were his best, and he committed himself to the Lord and proceeded to a new living level. The Bible states that *"The earnest prayer of a righteous man has great power and wonderful results"* **James 5:16 (TLB).** Mother White was intentional with her prayers, and she never gave up believing Dad would surrender his life to Christ.

Mom and I agreed that I would speak on behalf of the White family. Boy, was I nervous! I prayed to God that He would give me the words to say and that someone would be encouraged. The closer it got to my turn to speak, the sweatier the palms of my hands became. My heart was beating like crazy, and I could feel my mouth getting dry. I leaned over to Mom for comfort and encouragement. I knew if she told me I would be alright, I would be just fine!

The moderator called my name, and the butterflies fluttered in my stomach. The distance to the pulpit seemed a mile long. Slowly I walked toward the microphone. I thanked everyone for their attendance, visitation, calls, and food; I gave special acknowledgments to my family, church, close friends, and choir. Gradually, I began to feel more comfortable while speaking. The Holy Spirit had taken over, and eventually, there was no more fear.

After acknowledging everyone, I felt impressed by the Lord to share a story about my dad. I began to explain to the audience that while I was going through those years of trying to run from God, Dad loved me and hoped for the best for me. I'm sure he prayed for me the best he knew how. I knew Dad gave his life to Christ through our conversations. He stopped clubbing and chasing after women. Watching his new walk made a believer out of me. But one day, he said something to me that ultimately sealed the deal for me. Dad usually gave me money to spend any way I wanted for my birthday. But this time, he did something completely different. He said, ***"Shot, Daddy would like to buy you a dress for church!"***

"What!" I was stunned! I couldn't figure out why he would offer to buy me a dress for my birthday. It wasn't until a couple of days later that God revealed my daddy's reasoning. The Lord spoke to me and said, ***"Your father wanted to ask you to come back home to me, but he didn't know-how. So, he thought if he'd offer to buy you a dress to wear to church, you will come with him and surrender your life to me."*** I explained to the audience that this meant that our roles had suddenly reversed; instead of me trying to get Dad to accept Christ, he had become the evangelist, encouraging me to come back to Christ! Dad saw that I had switched places with him, and the path I was on wasn't right. I related to the audience that if God could change my Daddy, I knew he could do the same for anybody out there in the audience. The crowd stood, clapped for me, and started confirming and agreeing with my testimony with shouts of 'Hallelujah!'

As I walked down the stairs to my seat, I breathed a sigh of relief. I was so happy that moment was over. Just as I went to sit down, the Holy Spirit came upon me, and I began to dance before the Lord. All my life, I'd believed that God's presence commands praise. When I finally came to myself, I realized the whole church had erupted in a praise break! Mom sat clapping her hands, shaking her head, approving the outbreak of praise.

There were so many resolutions and cards, too many to read. But they were all acknowledged. Our pastor, my Father in the Lord, eulogized Dad by sharing stories and giving an invitation to accept Christ. We were extremely pleased with the entire service and the participants. We greeted family and friends after the funeral, making our way to the burial.

I was thankful to God for strengthening my mom through that tough time. She had been through adversities with Dad, but the victories outweighed them. She was quiet while we traveled to the gravesite, and I imagined she was trying to accept that the burial would signal the final moment of closure. My cousin and I held Mom's arms as we walked to be seated for the committal service. Our pastor braced himself to read the scripture and offer prayers for our family. I could see that he was hurting because he knew we were hurting. He loved Dad and had known him for years as well.

The committal service was now over; we placed roses on Dad's brown casket. We hugged those who came and watched them go to their cars. The funeral staff asked Mom if she was ready to leave, and her response was no. My heart sank while watching her stare at my dad's casket. Tears were rolling down both of our faces. I said, *"God, we need you now!"*

Mom turned to me and said, "I don't want to leave your daddy; the ground is too cold to leave him here." She wiped her eyes and turned back to look at the casket again.

For a few seconds, I had no response. Then, the Holy Spirit gave me words to say. I said, *"Mom, Daddy isn't going in the ground. That is just his shell, and his soul is with the Lord. He won't feel the effects of the cold."*

Mom looked at me for a moment, and then she said, "Baby, you are right. Your daddy is with the Lord." Gradually, we walked to the funeral car as Mom took one last glance at Dad's casket. She loved Clinton White, and he would be forever in her heart.

Chapter 5

Chapter 5
Adjusting To A New Way Of Life

We headed back to the church for the repast. It was a quiet ride in the car the funeral home had reserved for Mom and me, so it gave me a chance to reflect on the day's events. At that moment, I was proud of my family, who had come from both near and far. Their support had made this difficult situation somewhat bearable. During times of sadness, it's so uplifting to have your loved ones by your side. Dad had been a significant player in the Olympic-sized task of keeping his grandfather's children and their children together. I was incredibly thankful for my aunt. She had traveled a long way to be with us, and she had selflessly agreed to stay with us those three weeks of Dad's final days. While she was there, I could go to work every day without worrying about Mom taking care of my dad by herself. Even though the nurses and doctors were there to guarantee Dad's comfort, he looked for Mom to be sitting in the chair by his bed when he woke up each morning.

The repast afforded us time to thank those who assisted us said a kind word and participated in the program. We also reconnected with others we had not seen in a very long time. While we ate, we cried, laughed, and caught up on what was going on in the lives of our family and friends. When you're focused on taking care of a terminally ill family member, it's hard to find the time to stay in the loop. So, we spent that time renewing our connections. We hugged and kissed everybody; I was sorry to see them go.

As soon as we arrived home, I put Mom to bed. She put up a weak fight, but I looked her in her eyes and said, "Daddy told me to take care of you, and I think you need to get some rest. It's been a long emotional day." She gave in when she heard my explanation. I promised her that my cousin and I would adequately greet any visitor who would come by, make sure they had something to eat, place the food away, and clean up the kitchen. She smiled and leaned over toward me. She gently kissed my cheek, signifying that all was well. Thirty minutes later, when I stuck my head in her room to say goodnight, she was already breathing deeply with sleep.

Around six o'clock that evening, the doorbell finally stopped ringing. I was overwhelmed by the outpouring of love and concern shown by our community. But I was thoroughly exhausted, and a hot shower and the comfort of my bed sure sounded good to me. We took our showers, intending to go straight to bed. Of course, that didn't happen. We decided to do a quick recap of the day's events while eating some of the tasty food our friends and neighbors had brought. My cousin told me that I had actually preached my dad's funeral during the time of acknowledgments. I told him that I had done my best to keep my words short and simple, but I had gotten a little emotional while trying to explain how much my dad meant to me. Then, the power of God hit the room, and we found ourselves dancing, giving God the glory.

Finally, the clock hit midnight, and my cousin and I couldn't take it anymore. The bed was calling our names. We said our goodnights and staggered from the kitchen to our bedrooms. I checked on Mom one more time before turning out the light, and she was still sound asleep. I laid back on the pillow, preparing to talk to God before going to sleep. I don't remember that conversation at all.

The next day, I rose early to cook breakfast for Mom, just like Dad would have done. She enjoyed the eggs, the thick-cut bacon, and the toast I cooked for her. I'd stayed with Mom every night for the last three weeks, sharing her bed, and I needed to be close to her if she needed anything. I was determined to keep her from as much stress as possible.

After she finished her breakfast, I expected her to move to her favorite chair, read the newspaper, and reluctantly take a nap. To my surprise, she wanted to attend church. Shocked, I said okay, and I began to get her clothes together and help her get dressed for church. After making sure she was ready to go, I ran next door to my house to gather my clothes. I quickly showered and dressed. I believe Mom knew she had to do what she loved for the first time, knowing that Dad would never be by her side again. There was no use in putting it off going to church. Delaying it wouldn't change the fact that he wasn't coming back.

The church members were just as surprised to see us as I thought this would be too rough for Mom. It was more than a little awkward to be there without my dad, and the effects of his absence loomed larger than we thought. As hard as we tried, neither could hold back the tears. We did our best to praise God and focus on how good He had been to us. With that in mind, Mom and I made it through the service.

Later that day, I sat on the front porch, reflecting on how God had remained faithful, despite losing Dad. I closed my eyes, and I saw Dad in a beautiful light gold suit, gold

95

shoes, a gold shirt, and a gold tie. He was standing on a sidewalk made of pure gold, decorated with gold flowers. He looked so handsome, not a trace of any sickness. He smiled and said' ***"Shot, I love you and your mama, and I don't want you to worry about me; I'm with the Lord!"*** His voice seemed to echo, and an angelic presence surrounded the vision. I had never had a view of Heaven. Dad began to laugh, and I noticed that my neighbor, who had died fifteen years earlier, walked up to stand beside him. He was smiling gleamingly, and he was dressed the same way as my dad. Dad called my name again, saying, ***"Shot, God will take care of you and your mama. I love you all."***

When I came back to myself, I cried and praised God. I thanked Him for sending me confirmation and sharing His decision before the journey began with me. God didn't have to speak with me. He didn't have to help me process the events taking place. My gift as a Seer had benefited me, and I was genuinely grateful for all those things.

My employers were very kind to me during that difficult time in my life, and they allowed me to take extra time off to help Mom with other business matters. I learned lessons going through closing out all my dad's business affairs. There was no confusion with the names on the deeds to the houses, and we followed the necessary procedures to drop Dad's name from the documents adding both our names in the proper place without paying estate tax. I had heard some of the horror stories about spouses and children trying to acquire their deceased loved one's property. The Lord had once again gone before us to smooth out the rough place.

The days seemed long without Dad's joking, laughter, and thumping of my knuckles to show me that he loved me. Even the dog was trying to adjust to his absence. I noticed how Crystal, our dog, wouldn't leave Mom's side. It was as if she could feel Mom's sorrow. Crystal would follow us to the door when we prepared to leave the house, looking pitiful. So, we started taking her with us sometimes not to be left alone so much. Dad loved Crystal, and while he was sick, Crystal never left his side. I knew Dad would want us to do whatever we could to make Crystal happy.

It had been two weeks since we buried Daddy, and friends and family were still dropping by to check on us. We were shocked to find out that many of them had spoken privately with Dad during his last days. One of his buddies told us how far he and Dad went back. Their friendship started in the early seventies, and they would hit many clubs together up and down the coast. His friend would later maintain our houses' heating and air condition units. Once Dad found out that he didn't have long to live, he asked his friend always to make sure the A.C. units were always in excellent working condition. Another one of my friends shared that my dad had asked her to look out for me. Wow! Daddy loved us, so he did everything to make sure his family would survive his transition, and for that, I deeply love him to this day.

Before going back to work, I sat down with Mom to discuss how we would do life without Dad. I began to make plans for how she would get lunch while I was at work, when I would be there to prepare dinner for her, and which days we would be going out to eat. Her doctor's appointments remained the same, and she was comfortable driving herself there without me. We agreed that she would call me when she reached the doctor's office and again once she made it back home. That was a load off my shoulders. My work schedule would have made it extremely difficult to get the visits to the doctor.

While talking with Mom, I remembered Dad speaking to me exclusively about Mom's care. On his death bed, he had a special request for me. He asked me to promise him that I would lay my eyes on my mom every day. I promised him that I would gladly look out for her. I even took my agreement with Dad a step further. Although my house was right next door to my parent's home, I spent the nights with her so she wouldn't be alone all day and all night. I was sure she would wake up in a panic some nights if I didn't stay there with her. I didn't want her alone, grieving her beloved husband all day and night without me. It was important to me to comfort her whenever she needed me. I loved her with all my heart.

I only had a few days to gather my thoughts before returning to work. We closed out all of Dad's business matters, so the plan was for me to just lay around the house. Well, not so fast! I suddenly remembered that Dad had volunteered to host the 2000 Family Reunion. I jumped up from the sofa and said, "Mom, we need to start planning for the 2000 reunion!"

Mom looked up at me and said, "You have got to be kidding me, right? There is no way we can host the reunion without your father!"

I dropped my head and told her, "Mom, I know it's a lot of work, but we must finish what Daddy started. I believe God will be with us to host a reunion; the family will never forget."

Mom looked at me with doubt, but she said, "You're right. God wants us to finish what your Daddy started." Planning for the White Family Reunion started the very next day. The more I thought about all the work ahead of us, the more I realized that keeping Mom busy was what she needed. It helped us to keep our minds off our grief. I thanked God for the diversion, all the planning and work would provide.

Mom and I started making phone calls to different hotels, searching for the best deals on venues large enough to accommodate our family. While visiting the Marriot Hotel, the event coordinator offered us great food choices and room rates. After speaking with her and comparing her quote with some of the other hotels, we knew this was the right venue for the White Family Reunion 2000. Within days, we mailed out the reunion information to all our family. With the help of our local family, we were determined to make that reunion one of the best family gatherings ever. I wondered if Dad knew we would need that at that particular time. After all, he had always planned for the future.

As I prepared to return to work, I hid my struggles and grief from Mom. I felt like I couldn't put any more burdens on her. But I also knew my Mom was a Seer, and I couldn't hide anything from her for long. Her discernment level was sharp, so even if I hadn't shared how much my heart ached, she was still aware of it, and she was faithfully praying for me. My co-workers showed compassion and concern during my first day back to work. They hugged me continuously, and some of them even cried with me as they asked what they could do to help me get back on track at work. I was grateful for their support.

It was the fourth quarter, which meant hiring seasonal employees for the Christmas Holidays. While I took care of my family, my manager hired two new hires for my department. My job was to train them and prepare them for the biggest day in retail after Thanksgiving. I had beautiful inventory, and I was itching to sell as much jewelry as possible. My goal was to make my manager and district manager proud of our numbers from fulfilling our quota. There wasn't a lot of time to learn the product and how to sell it, but we would do a crash course. One of the new employees was available during the day, so I trained her when I worked the day shift. The other new hire had a day job and worked with us during the evenings and weekends.

The fourth quarter is always fascinating because you can have new seasonal items for the customers. Our inventory would balloon considerably, and we had adjustments made to present it properly. You always took a chance when hiring new people. You could hope they were honest, not easily intimidated, and could maneuver as a commissioned salesperson. Commissioned salespeople can be vicious, competitive, and even cutthroat at times. There was no room for passiveness. Much to my excitement, the new hires did well, and they learned quickly. I felt their addition to my team would benefit me greatly.

One of the new hires was new to the area, and her husband arrived here six months earlier on a military assignment. They were stationed here for four years. She didn't know about our small cities that linked together. Over time, we became friends, and I eventually met her husband. He was charming and easy to be around. He loved to cook, and sometimes he would tell his wife to invite me over to dinner. His specialty was ribs, baked beans, and corn! It tasted just like the barbeque cooked on the side of the road by a man who never owned a restaurant but should have. I'm not usually a smacker when I eat, but I'm almost sure I smacked a couple of times while eating his cooking.

The fourth quarter ended, and we celebrated that our department had been successful. The entire store made its plan, and the district acknowledged us. Our store manager received a plaque in honor of his leadership. The amazing thing was that our store manager had fallen ill at the beginning of December. He had become the team leader precisely one year before that time. He received a diagnosis of brain cancer six months before taking the position of senior management. I remember the day he introduced himself to us at a staff meeting. He was a Christian and shared his faith with us. He didn't want us to worry about his health because his trust was in Jesus.

I thought about it in hindsight, and I believed he was strategically sent to our store to transform us into winners. He would pray over the lunches served at our meetings, and he invited me to pray as a believer in Jesus Christ. He brought God into our environment, which was the change we needed. Our morale had been low, and our plan numbers showed it. We ranked 23rd out of 25 stores when he came to us. But because of our store manager's incredible leadership, we finished the year at number one in our district.

In January, we cleaned up from the fourth quarter. Our staff held meetings every Monday to discuss issues and make plans for weeks and months. Our store manager remained hospitalized, but the doctors continued relaying positive reports, and we expected him to be healthy enough to return to work eventually.

God visited me in a night vision after the news of his improving health from his doctors. I saw all the managers sitting in our meeting room. The wall opened while discussing store matters, and I saw a beautiful boat floating toward us. The water was like no water I'd ever seen before. It was clear, brightly beautiful, and alive. As the water moved the boat closer to us, I recognized my store manager standing on the ship's deck, smiling, looking perfectly healthy. Suddenly, he walked on water towards me and said, ***"I've enjoyed my time here as the store manager. You all embraced me, and for that, I'm grateful. But my time here with you is up, and I will not be returning."*** He asked me to tell everyone that he loved them, encouraging them to continue to do great things. Then he turned around slowly and boarded the boat again, the waves took it away, and the wall closed.

I wrestled with what I should do with this truth. I had been with the Lord long enough to know when He shared His heart, that was absolute. The following week, in our staff meeting, they talked about the doctor's positive report and how happy our store manager's return would be. At the end of our time together, every manager was given a chance to voice their concerns or opinions. That day, I was seated in the last chair, unintentionally. When I realized that I was sitting there because God wanted me to share the truth of our reality, butterflies took flight in my stomach, and my palms began to sweat. When it was finally my turn to speak, I fought to find the courage to give them the Lord's report. Gradually, I found my voice talking above a whisper. Everyone looked and listened as if they knew I had an important message for them. I asked them to excuse my tears as I shared our store manager's words from the night vision.

My voice began to tremble, and my palms were sweaty. Most of the team members knew I attended church, but they weren't aware of how God showed me present and past events through dreams and visions. At that time, my current soft-line manager was the only one who had experienced the Seer call upon my life. About six months before our store manager fell ill, she took a trip to New York. Two days before she left, I approached her and asked her to pray for her safety. I explained that God showed me the plane experiencing hefty turbulence. The vision revealed that the pilot struggled to get the plane's speed to a safe velocity. The airplane was shaking and moving up and down violently. The passengers were screaming as the pilot struggled to navigate to plane to safety. But I told my manager that everything would be alright because I had prayed for her safe return home.

A week later, after returning from her vacation, she found me and told me that everything God showed me about her trip happened. She described how the plane was seemingly out of control, and everyone was screaming. My boss also said that the only thing that helped her remain calm was remembering our conversation and praying on her behalf. She was able to rest in the knowledge that the unusual turbulence wasn't going to propose a threat to their lives.

I began to share God's vision concerning our store manager with all eyes on me. Reluctantly, I let them know that he would not be coming back to work with us. Some of my colleagues responded by reminding us that we had just gotten an encouraging doctor's report that said he would be able to return to work within a couple of months. They desperately wanted to believe the good news that his health

103

was improving. With tears streaming down my face, I explained that I was also very hopeful when I heard the doctor's report. But a few days after receiving that report, God had shown me that His will was for our store manager to leave this world and rest in the arms of Jesus.

I managed to say that I was heartbroken through my tears, but I knew God's will is sovereign, even when we don't understand it. Some team members began to cry and speak well of our store manager. Everyone knew he was special, a remarkable leader, and a man of great faith. After coming to terms with God's decision, we discussed the district award that he hadn't had a chance to receive yet. We were waiting for his return to work to present the award and throw a big party to celebrate his return and recognize his accomplishments. We began to discuss how best to present the award, and the consensus of the room was that it would be best to hand-deliver the plaque. Unanimously, they voted for me to take the district award to our store manager. What a tremendous honor bestowed on me, and I did not take it lightly. That day, we ended our meeting with me, for the first time, praying for the family's strength and ours as well.

After work, I went home to check on Mom. I shared with her the vision and God's instructions to share it with my co-workers. It was emotionally challenging because our store manager was a type of Deliverer and Father figure in my eyes. We hadn't thrived as much as we should have under the past leadership. By the time the district manager sent us a new manager, the store was in chaos, and the store's morale was at an all-time low. It was a no-brainer when we were ranked almost dead last out of twenty-five stores in the district. The word that our store manager would soon transition was tough to swallow. I hadn't finished processing the loss of my dad, and I was still grieving. The thought of losing two valuable male figures within a few months was simply devastating.

Mom and I traveled to the hospital to present the district award to our well-deserving store manager a week later. While driving to the hospital, Mom and I talked about letting people know how much they mean to you while they can still hear you. I had prepared a few words I wanted to share with our store manager on behalf of his team. We arrived at the hospital and met his beautiful wife in the waiting room on his floor. She briefed us on his condition and told us what to expect when we entered the hospital room. Mom chose to stay in the waiting room, which I thought was best. She was still grieving the loss of her beloved husband, and the sights and sounds of the hospital room threatened to reopen a wound that was already struggling to heal.

In preparing for this visit, I had asked God to let my words be soothing and appropriate. I wanted my store manager to feel the heart of his managers. I walked into the room, and immediately my store manager smiled and yelled my name! He was so happy to see me, and he reached out for my hand. It was such a touching moment; I almost lost my composure. He began to talk about the goodness of God, and I could feel the presence of God in the room. It was evident that my store manager was at peace regardless of what would happen.

I began to share the reason I was there. I tried very hard to keep the tears from flowing, but before I knew it, the front of my shirt was wet with tears. I expressed that God sent him to our store to love us and resurrect us. His faith in God had shifted the atmosphere, and for the first time, people felt free to talk about their faith. I told him that he was the sunshine we needed. His role as a strong, loving leader had made the difference.

I picked up the plaque and showed him the reward for his labor. He reached out and touched the award with tears in his eyes. He expressed that we were like his children, and he loved us dearly. He asked me to give everyone a big hug and share his love and appreciation. I sat there by his bed, reminiscing about the good times shared as a team. I didn't want to stay too long. I could tell that he was in great pain as he lifted his head to talk to me. I hugged his wife, letting her know that I would keep them in my prayers, and she could call me if they needed anything.

As I was leaving, my store manager said, **"Hey, don't you leave without hugging my neck!"** I knew he was giving me his final goodbye. I was a total wipe-out by then, but he comforted me by saying, "I am in the arms of Jesus." I left the hospital feeling that I had done my best to represent our store.

Two weeks later, our store manager died. Although I knew he was transitioning and I had done what I could to prepare the others, it was still emotionally challenging. Managers from other stores volunteered to work our shifts so everyone could attend our leader's funeral. The funeral location was an hour away, and the long drive gave us time to prepare ourselves. There was special seating reserved for us. We were acknowledged as his team and asked to stand. I think we all kind of lost it at that moment. Our Assistant Store Manager shared reflections on behalf of all of us. I'll never forget the quality of our Store Manager's leadership. He showed us that you could give life to a dead situation with hard work and instructions. On the way home, my co-worker and I shared personal memories of our Store Manager, and it seemed to help our pain.

Our first meeting after his funeral was quiet and reflective. We all decided to continue saying grace over our lunch every Monday, just like we had done when he was still with us. We thought we should keep our Store Manager's legacy alive. Some of my co-workers commended me for having the strength to share our Store Manager's outcome when the reports were pointing towards a full recovery. I responded that God had strengthened me and given me the courage to communicate His will concerning the matter. I wanted them to know the Seer gift was from the Lord, and I could take no credit for my ability.

Now, I had to deal with the fact that two great leaders had met their appointment with death. They both had an impact on my life. From the time I entered this world, my natural Father always believed in me and taught me principles that are valid today. Years after his death, he is relevant in my thoughts and actions. Clinton White is imprinted in my heart permanently.

For a year and a half, my store manager rallied and empowered leaders who had lost their passion. He did just that and resurrected that our faith in God was vital to our success. No manager ever mixed their spiritual views with leading. It was a success, and I'll never forget our beloved Store Manager. I'm thankful God afforded me a chance to have these people part of my life. What treasures were given to me by God? When people leave your life, you honor them by practicing their contributions with others. Legacies become alive when a person transitions from this life. I will always love them.

Chapter 6

Chapter 6
Entanglement

It had been months since the seasonal help had left my department to find other jobs. One day, I received a call from my old employee's husband. He was going out of town on a military assignment within the next two weeks and wanted to know if I would look out for his wife while he was away. He explained that sometimes she would experience pain from fibroid tumors, and he wasn't comfortable leaving her alone while he was away on duty. At that point, I wasn't sure if I could handle any more responsibility. Emotionally, I was still adjusting to the loss of my father and the unexpected passing of my store manager. The thought of taking on something else weighed heavily on my mind. But because he had been so very welcoming to me, I decided to agree to watch out for his wife and ease his mind while he was away. The next day, his wife called me and told me how happy she was that I had said yes to her husband's request.

I told Mom about her husband's request. I invited my former employee to come by the house to meet Mom, and we all went to dinner together. All my friends adored Mom, and she was no different. We had a great time laughing and talking as she told us about her mother and her siblings. No matter where you come from, southern mamas are pretty much the same. Everybody they spend time with will eventually become their child. So, it didn't surprise me when Mom invited the young lady to go with us to see a stage play in three weeks. She was excited to be included and said yes without giving it any thought.

Time went by quickly, and before I knew it, her husband contacted me again the day before his unit left for his weekend duty commitment. I assured him that I would look out for his wife and call him if there was an emergency.

I couldn't believe it! It hadn't been twenty-four hours since her husband left, and she began to experience severe pain. She called me and asked me to take her to the emergency room. I was thirty minutes away from her, so I rushed to get there and get her to the hospital. She decided to wait for a diagnosis before calling her husband. She told me this wasn't the first time she needed to go to the emergency room for this issue. While waiting for her test results, they gave her pain meds to ease her discomfort. I desperately wanted to call her husband to let him know we were at the emergency room like I had promised. I guess this had been the norm for her for so long; she knew the routine. She asked me to wait with her for the doctor's report, then call her husband.

I finally agreed it might be best to wait until we had some information to give her husband. I didn't want to alarm him unnecessarily. So, I waited anxiously with her, hoping we'd know something soon. Staying in the ER could be extended by hours on a Friday night, and I was thankful her results came back in a couple of hours. While the doctor explained her test results, I listened very attentively. I wanted to know all the details of what I was talking about when I finally called her husband.

Since her last ER visit, the results showed that the tumors had grown significantly. The doctor suggested surgically removing the tumors to alleviate the pain. She sighed with tears; she didn't want to have the surgery. I consoled her as best as I could, trying to convince her it was best so she wouldn't need to visit the ER periodically.

The doctor signed her release papers, quickly wrote a prescription for pain medicine for her, and walked out of the room. I walked over to the phone to call her husband's commander to inform him of her ER visit. Once I had the commander on the line, I explained who I was and why I needed to speak with one of his soldiers. When her husband finally got to the phone, I explained what was happening and what the doctor suggested. While talking with him, I turned to check and see if she wanted to speak with her husband.

As I began to ask her if she felt like talking on the phone, I saw a silhouette of something coming through the ceiling, and it appeared to have dissolved itself into my friend's body. It had been a long day, and I had been under a lot of stress. Were my eyes fooling me? I rubbed my eyes and just tried to forget what I saw. I asked her if she wanted to speak with her husband. Surprisingly, she said she didn't want to talk with him. I quickly made up an excuse for not putting her on the phone and told her husband that I would make sure she got home safely, and we would call him back later. After he hung up, she asked me to call her mother to inform her of the ER visit and the test results. I agreed to do that, but I was concerned by her refusal to speak with her husband.

I packed up her things, and we headed to the 24-hour pharmacy and home. During the drive, she thanked me for taking her to the emergency room, calling her husband and family, and being so kind to her. I didn't view my help as a sacrifice; she had no friends or family here, so it was the least I could do. Besides, I had made a promise to her husband.

I thought it would be good to stop at a drive-thru and pick up something for both of us to eat. I knew with taking pain medicine, she would need to eat, and I wasn't sure if she had food already prepared at her house. After arriving at her townhouse, I helped her get settled, put her food close by her, and gave her the pain medicine. While I was getting things ready for her, she asked if I would play a new cd she'd purchased. I wasn't listening to secular music at that time, so I had no idea of the artist or his music. The first song started to play, and the lyrics immediately caught my attention. The music had a smooth vibe, and I thought it wasn't half bad. The song's title was "I Wish I Never Met Her." I stood still and listened to the soulful, sensual longing in the singer's voice. When I looked up, she was singing along and staring at me. The moment was awkward and unsettling. Then she took a bite of her burger and explained that she and her husband were not on the best terms.

I was altogether dumbfounded; they seemed to have a great relationship. I encouraged my friend to keep working on her marriage, and I explained that all relationships go through struggles from time to time. I assured her that everything would be alright. She didn't seem too enthusiastic about the possibilities, but I attributed that to the pain medicines. The song "I Wish I Never Met Her" played every time we were together from that day on. It was as if she was trying to send me a subliminal message.

Her husband's unit was home by that Sunday night. He called to thank me, telling me how much he appreciated everything I had done while he was away. I told him it was okay. I would have wanted someone to do the same for me. A couple of days went by, and the pain my friend had been experiencing was gone. Her husband invited me over the following Friday night for dinner. Surprisingly enough, we had a great time. We all laughed at their stories about their experiences in other cities. It was hard to believe they weren't getting along. The next day, she and I caught a movie together and grabbed a burger afterward. Occasionally, I wondered about the image I'd seen while talking to her husband on the phone. I felt like I couldn't ask her if she had experienced anything out of the ordinary while we were in the ER. So, I just kept it to myself.

I invited her to come to church with Mom and me. I warned her that we were Pentecostals, and we could get loud and look peculiar. I didn't want to scare her, and I felt obligated to give her a short briefing before she experienced it firsthand. I also shared with her that I was a minister and a musician. I told her that I had recently lost my father, and I didn't want her caught off guard if someone at church mentioned his death. We all went to dinner after church. She said the singing was impressive. Of course, I gave her a brief history of the choir and explained how my Father in the Lord played for us and how we were seasoned singers and musicians.

After church, my friend called and asked if I were available to speak with her. She said she had something important to discuss with me. I told her I was free at the moment. I noticed that there was a distinct hint of concern in her voice. As I made myself comfortable at the kitchen counter, I couldn't help but wonder what was going on. Maybe she and her husband had argued, and she was upset, or she just needed somebody to hear her frustrations.

Well, her relationship with her husband was the furthest thing from her mind. What she told me threw me for a loop! She explained how she had started to experience emotions for me while working for me, knowing it wasn't right. At first, she thought it was something she was going through because of her difficulties in her marriage. She was sure it would pass, but then she realized that her feeling wasn't going away but was increasing.

She shared that she dreamed about us being married to each other. She planned to discontinue our friendship rather than risk ruining our relationship by making unwanted advances toward me.

I felt like I was in a daze. For a moment, I couldn't even speak. I thought to myself, "What in the world happened?" In my mind, the residue of my past was gone. I couldn't believe what my ears heard. Finally, my voice returned to me, and I stumbled over a few questions. "Did I do something to make you feel this way?" I asked. She confirmed that I hadn't done anything to spark her feelings. She confessed that she was puzzled about how her emotions could have gotten so out of control. She never had a same-sex attraction in her life. So, it was all very new to her, and she was understandably afraid. I tried to ease her by telling her that we could talk about it later. I was hoping that this was just a big mistake the whole time. Her confession had stunned me entirely.

I desperately needed to think things through. As I moved from the kitchen counter to my lazy boy chair, I began to reflect on our visit to the ER. I concluded that God had shown me an image of lust that the enemy sent to intensify her feelings for me. How could I have missed this? Was I attracted to her and in denial of my feelings?

I had never shared with her that I once lived as a lesbian, nor did I ever mention that I was a dreamer. Although, whenever my flesh failed me in the past, I convinced myself that we could remain friends, if we were cautious, and unfortunately, that never worked.

I called her the next day, apologizing that she was experiencing those emotions. I couldn't bring myself to tell her about my past experiences. Guilt was settling in, making me feel like it was my fault. I expressed that I felt like she would be okay, and this was just a phase she was going through. I knew this was more than just a phase, and I was in trouble.

I began to limit my conversations with her, convincing myself that I was doing the right thing. Usually, I would see her on the weekends with her husband or have lunch at a restaurant with her, or we would just catch a movie together. I decided against seeing her the weekend after she confessed her interest in me, and she never asked any questions.

The following weekend, while her husband was away on duty, the stage play Mom and I invited her to started. We'd waited two whole months to see this play, and we were excited to be going, finally. Mom and I waited for her to arrive at my house. When she finally arrived, the three of us got in the car and headed out of town to see the play. I felt a little uncomfortable, wondering if God had shown Mom that I was playing with fire.

While driving, the Lord began to speak. He said, *"You're in danger and I sent the dream to her to warn you."* I didn't talk much on the ride over because I was wrestling with my soul.

When the play ended, we headed back home. We ate before the event to avoid long lines knowing it would be too late to find decent food on the road after the play was over. We talked about how well the actors performed, and it was definitely worth the two-month wait. Before too long, I pulled into my driveway. We said our hurried and awkward goodnights; my friend started her car and waved as she backed out of the driveway.

I took Mom into the house and helped her prepare for bed. Even though we went through the motions of getting ready for bed, Mother White went straight to her computer once she had on her nightgown. She wanted to chat with her friends about the play and make quick notes on the outline we'd created for the family reunion. Mom liked to jot down things that were fresh in her mind. I was happy she had

115

something to do while still getting used to Dad not being with her. I kissed her on her forehead as I headed to shower.

I waited for my friend to call to make sure she had gotten home safely. We didn't talk much that night, but I knew that a soul tie was between us. My mind started telling me I wasn't delivered, and I would always be a lesbian. I wanted to fight, but I was in too deep. I should have chosen my freedom while I had the strength. God had done His part again to warn me of failure. Again, I decided not to do the right thing for myself. The minute I heard that she cared for me, I should have saved her and myself by parting ways.

At this point, my thoughts condemned me, and I could hardly pray. It had been three hard-fought years of walking in freedom from my past. My mind could not comprehend going back to experience the heartache again. I was living my life for Jesus, and I was content. I had heard "once gay, always gay." It kept ringing in my head. Although I was struggling and a fall seemed to be just around the corner, I refused to believe that phrase was absolute.

She called the next day asking if she could bring me lunch, and I told her she could, even though the Holy Spirit continued to counsel me, urging me to avoid the trap of my flesh. There is one thing I am sure of; the Holy Spirit never stops trying, and He continuously tries to re-direct our footsteps. How could He be so patient with me, knowing that my state of mind was "whatever happens, happens" at that point?

Nervously, I waited for the knock at the door. When it came, I yelled, "The door is open!" I was in the kitchen, putting ice in our glasses and getting the sodas out of the fridge. We sat at the kitchen table, eating and talking about the play. Before we knew it, an hour had passed. She wanted to say hello to Mom before she left and headed back home. That was a great idea, and Mom was so happy she'd stopped.

We both stood on the porch, waving as she drove away. Disaster averted!

Even though nothing had happened, my mind was full of thoughts I'd worked hard to remove from my daily life. I had let myself go to a dangerous place. After hearing her say that I hadn't done anything to influence or encourage her feelings for me, I desperately wanted to believe my friend. Although I didn't want to admit it, I was flattered by her emotions for me. Being pursued can stroke your ego if you're not careful. I mulled the whole situation over and over in my head. Maybe I was in denial and wanted her as much as she wanted me.

Because the conviction of the Lord would not allow me to settle in my feelings, I began to have sleepless nights. I could hear the Holy Spirit saying, ***"Don't throw away the three years you've worked so hard to obtain. You haven't gone too far to turn around!"***

I began to cry and tell the Lord how sorry I was that I hadn't done what I knew to do at her confession. I started adjusting and limiting our time on the phone, no longer spending time together eating out or going to the movies.

I started feeling better, but I missed her laughter, conversations, and movie nights together. She told me she understood why we needed to distance ourselves from each other, and we had to do whatever we could to keep us from crossing the line.

One Sunday evening, I was relaxing in my recliner, watching one of my favorite shows. Mom and I had attended church together earlier that morning, and after dining out, she went to her house for a nap. I went to my house to unwind and get my things ready for work the next day. I planned to go back to Mom's house when it got dark. My eyes were getting heavy when I heard a knock at my front door; I wondered who it could be because I wasn't expecting any visitors. From the comfort of my chair, I asked who it was with a loud voice. I heard the name, and it shocked me. She had traveled to see me, unannounced. Even though she had come unannounced and uninvited, I was happy to see her. She asked if she could come in for a few minutes from the porch. She explained that her husband was away, and she was taking a Sunday drive and thought she'd drop by to say hello.

In my heart, I knew I should not have asked her in. I should have stepped out onto the front porch, sat down in the warmth of the evening sun, and talked with her. I was in denial about how strong my feelings were for her. We sat at the dining room table, making small talk. I asked all those pointless questions. How are things going on her job? Is her relationship better with her husband? What had she been doing? She began to say she missed working with my team and was so bored with everything.

I smiled and agreed that we were a terrific team. Then I inquired more about the marriage, asking if counseling could help resolve the issues. To my surprise, the answer was not what I expected. At first, my friend just shrugged off my question. Then, she began to say that she no longer cared about solving their problems with a distant look. My response was to tell her that I was sorry things between them weren't getting better. I tried to assure her that it would take some time, but it would eventually be better. I spoke those words. I heard myself say them. They even sounded sincere to my ears. But to be honest, a part of me was happy that they were still struggling in their marriage.

When I realized that I felt overjoyed at the idea of their marriage not going well, I quickly changed the subject and asked her if she wanted a soda. I invited her to sit on the couch and watch my favorite shows with me. What had started as a quick stop to say hello, turned into a couple of shared hours? We laughed and reminisced about our favorite shows and completely lost track of time. When I realized we'd been sitting there so long, I awkwardly suggested that she go home so she could be there by the time her husband returned from duty.

While slipping on my flip-flops, she turned to me and said, "I know you love the Lord. I'm not right for you as a friend because my emotions have taken me to where I've never been. Having an attraction for another female has never happened to me before. I'm scared, but I can't act as if I don't know what I'm feeling. I've fallen in love with you, and I want to be with you." Tears were streaming down her face. I didn't know what to say, but I couldn't take my eyes off her. She continued talking, telling me that the real reason for her visit was that she needed to say to me how she felt about me. "I can't pretend that I don't love you anymore!" By that time, she was sobbing uncontrollably.

I had no words for a few seconds, and I battled for a minute about what I should say or do next. I got up quickly, left the room, and came back with a box of Kleenex. I dried her tears with shaky hands and a tissue. I told her I was sorry for the thoughts and feelings she had experienced. I explained why she was feeling the way she was feeling. I also told her my past and revealed that I am a Seer. I admitted that the Lord warned me about our situation through her dreams. I began to cry because, even though I knew it was dangerously wrong, my soul wanted to be with her just as much as she wanted to be with me. I embraced her, knowing that she wouldn't be able to resist or overcome her desire for me. That day we became intimate, and I admitted that I loved her too.

After she left that evening, I tried to get myself together. I felt so guilty and ashamed that I didn't take the necessary actions to stop our relationship from developing and heading full steam in the wrong direction. I repented to the Lord, but I knew it would take some time to unravel my soul from hers. Still, I was determined not to give up this time. Owning up to the fact that I had given in to my desires was painful. Since God had brought me out three years earlier, I had been able to remain focused and to walk out my destiny. Now, I had just wiped out all the progress I'd made.

The following day, I was still stunned by my behavior, and it felt as if my emotions were leading me again. While at work, I couldn't get beyond the memory of our evening together. I tried to cast them down, but I had allowed myself to become too powerless. It was as if the enemy was laughing at me and mocking me simultaneously. What could I say? I wanted to be with her as much as she wanted to be with me. She hadn't done anything that wasn't familiar. I couldn't blame this on the devil. I had the tools I needed to escape, but I chose to be entangled and satisfy my desires.

After work, I immediately went home to check on my mom. I wanted to make sure she was doing okay and eating throughout the day. My conscience weighed me down with guilt, and I was too ashamed to be around her for long. God hid nothing from Mother White concerning her family. Sensing that something wasn't right, she asked if everything was okay with me. I tried hard, but I just wasn't myself, and she knew her child was troubled.

I decided to go home and sit in my lazy boy chair, staring at the television. My phone rang while I was sitting there, and I saw my friend's name on the caller ID. I reluctantly picked up the phone to answer, but I couldn't click the button to answer the call. I didn't know what to say, and nothing came to my mind. I softly placed the phone back on the receiver and started cleaning the house and doing other chores. I needed to get her off my mind. A few hours later, the phone rang again. This time, I responded to her call.

We were both quiet at first, neither knowing what to say to the other. I asked how was it going? She told me that all day her thoughts were on us. She had been trying to figure out how we should move from that point, and I wondered the same thing. I said, "Making better choices because we've experienced intimacy, and that place is hard to leave." She agreed.

Later that week, her husband invited me to lunch on Saturday. That Saturday came, and I found myself sitting across the table from them. Her husband informed me that his wife's pain had become excruciating, and her fibroid tumor surgery was scheduled for two months away. He also told me that his military unit would be gone for three weeks, and he would need me to be with my friend while she recovered.

While listening to him, my conscience was beating me up the entire time. If he only knew that we weren't just friends, but lovers, there's no telling what he would have done. He certainly wouldn't have trusted me to care for her while he was away on duty. Of course, I told him, yes, and I'd take excellent care of her while he was away. She sat there smiling at me the whole time, just as if she didn't have any guilt or shame. I could barely look at her husband in his face. After lunch, I decided to leave; I couldn't take it anymore, knowing that I was in love with his wife and sleeping with her.

My friend was extremely excited, knowing that we would have more time together while her husband was away serving his country. While driving home, my mind was all over the place. She called to see if I was okay because I had left right after lunch was over. I tried to explain how bad I felt that I was pretending only to be her friend, knowing how much her husband trusted me. She seemed not to be bothered or to be experiencing any guilt. She tried to convince me that she and her husband had discussed divorce, and there would be no reconciliation between them. The truth was that they were still married. We were having an illicit affair, and I was not coping well emotionally or spiritually.

My schedule only involved taking care of Mom. Nothing would come before that task. Every plan centered around what I needed to do for my mom. My friend was responsible for making sure her husband had no reason to be suspicious of us. We squeezed out time for lunches, watched a movie, and spent time together at my house. The guilt I once felt was fading as we continued to see each other more often. I'd given up repenting because I knew I didn't want to end the relationship. The Holy Spirit didn't leave me, though; I just refused the instructions He gave me so I could continue in our relationship.

One Sunday evening, my friend came over with food for our dinner. I noticed that she wasn't cheerful, so I asked if she was alright. She looked at me with tears and said she had a dream the night before. Somehow, I already knew this wasn't good, and God was up to doing what He does best. He was wrecking and tearing up stuff for my good.

Anxiously, I asked what she had seen in the vision. My friend shared that in her dream Mom, myself, and she were attending church together. She told me that I was sitting in the pulpit, crying. While I sat there crying, my lips were silently moving, and no one could hear what I was saying. God told her that our relationship had to end, and it was too much for me to handle. He shared that His Hand was upon my life for ministry.

I dropped my head and hugged her, and we cried together, understanding that what we shared was coming to an end. I wasn't shocked by her vision. I knew God had a season when He would step in and make sure I surrendered my life again. He had already shown me that He would do what's best for me when His patience had become exhausted while waiting for me.

We sat on my couch for a few hours as she laid her head on my shoulder. Quietly, we sniffed and wiped each other's tears. So many thoughts were running through my head. This relationship seemed different from my past relationships. Although I had only known her for eight months, the five months we had spent together as lovers seemed like years. Our bond grew fast in a short time. I knew it would be challenging to pull her from my soul, and it would take everything within me. For sure, I knew I couldn't do it on my own. She said she couldn't bear the thought of being in the way of ministry and ruining my life. I did my best to explain to her that it wasn't her fault and that God used her to get to me.

It was getting late, so my friend gathered her things, and I gave her the leftover food for her next day's lunch. We held hands as we walked to the door. She stopped, hugged me, and kissed me on my cheek. I told her that I loved her enough to let her go. We stood there for a few moments, and I finally got the strength to open the door to let her leave. My heart was hurting, but I couldn't blame anyone else for my pain.

I showered and went over to Mom's house to stay with her. I tried my best to act as if nothing was going on with me. Mom could see through dirty water if God wanted her to.

I didn't want her to know that I had been crying, so I pretended to use Noxzema to clean my face while in the bathroom. I even tried to hum and sing while letting the water run in the sink. Somehow, I knew I wasn't fooling Mom.

After asking her if she needed anything, I climbed into bed and turned my back on her so she couldn't see my face. She touched my back and said, "Everything will be alright."

I flipped over onto my back, staring straight up at the ceiling. "Yes, ma'am. I love you, Mom. Goodnight", I managed to mumble out through pretend yawns. I turned my face to the wall, and the tears fell while the pain was squeezing everything out of me. At that moment, I knew she was aware of my failure and my need for restoration.

There was no communication between my friend and me for a whole week. That was a long hard week, but we had to start somewhere. Later, we decided to spend a Saturday evening together, for the last time. My heart ached, but I felt like I just wanted to see her one more time. That Saturday, waiting for her to arrive to go to dinner, I started to feel a little sick. Maybe my stomach was a little upset because of the stress.

My phone began to ring, and the caller ID announced that it was my friend. Why would she be calling me unless something happened? I asked if she was okay and where she was, and she answered, "I'm okay." She then told me that she was sitting outside my house in her car. I thought to myself, this is strange.

As I approached the vehicle, she rolled down the window and said, "I don't think it's a good idea to spend the evening together." Confused and a little hurt, I asked what made her change her mind. She explained that she thought we would continue our relationship if we didn't bring closure to it right then. I knew she was right, but it didn't stop the hurt I felt.

I simply said "Okay" and turned around and walked back to my house. Five minutes later, she called, and I didn't answer. I laid down on my couch, and the tears wouldn't stop flowing. If I didn't know how much God loved me, this was the overwhelming proof. Here I was again at a point in my life where I had given in to temptation and pleased my flesh. It had been nine months since the death of my father. I began to take an assessment of my spiritual life since his death. I had to retrace my steps to pinpoint exactly where my soul began to say 'yes' to my past bondage. I needed to address my soul and recover, continuing the life of freedom I received from Christ.

With my heart broken into pieces, I wanted desperately to get my life back as I had known it before I had said yes to the things that had wrecked my life. I couldn't deny that I decided to get involved in a relationship, knowing the consequences of my actions. I was taking a chance to be in control, leaving when ready. The tables were the exact opposite. I didn't want to end our relationship, but God took it out of my hands. I screamed because it felt as though God ripped my heart from my soul. I asked God to heal my soul and my emotions. I never made it to bed, and I cried myself to sleep on Mom's couch.

The following day, I prepared breakfast for Mom before church. I tried to be my jolly self, but I knew God had shown her that I was troubled. I went back to my house to get dressed. Once inside the doorway, I fell to my knees. The only words I could say were, ***"God, help me again! Please! Free me from the pain of my broken heart!"*** My brokenness seemed overwhelming, but I knew worship was the medicine I so desperately needed.

The service began as the praise team ushered us into the presence of God. I barely made it through the first song, and I laid on the floor while God was working on me, repairing the damage I'd done.

The following week, I started consecrating to help my mind, body, and spirit realign with God. As each day passed, I felt healing, and strength being added to me. I didn't realize just how weak I'd become. There was no one to blame for my decisions. But I learned the importance of maintaining my spiritual strength while helping others. I asked the Lord, where did I fail? He answered, *"After your father's death, you ministered to others and never replenished. When temptation presented itself, you didn't have the strength to resist."* It was tough to hear that.

Out of the blue, one Monday morning, I was surprised to see my friend walk through the door at my job. I had not been answering or returning her calls, nor had I visited her in over a month. It was awkward but pleasant. She invited me to lunch, but I declined. I still loved her, but my heart and soul had come a long way, and I wasn't going to jeopardize my progress. Her visit was about the scheduled removal of her fibroids. She reminded me of her husband's request, and she wanted to know if I'd still consider being with her husband during her surgery. Her godfather was replacing me and would be with her after the surgery. I'd already consented to be with her husband during the operation, so I said yes, I'd be there. After confirming that I'd still be there for her, I politely thanked her for stopping by and told her I needed to get back to work. To be honest, I had nowhere to go, but I needed to get away from her. This time, I wasn't giving myself a chance to have second thoughts about disconnecting.

The procedure was less than two weeks away, and I had already arranged to be off from work, so there would be no conflict. The closer it got to the date, the more nervous I became, and I understood how necessary it was to remain prayerful and focused. I confirmed the time and place of the surgery with my friend's husband, and he was so happy. I would pray over the whole situation, but he had no clue about the relationship I shared with his wife.

126

I arrived at the hospital and met them in the waiting room. The nurses took her back and prepared her for the surgery. After thirty minutes went by, her husband and I could see her. I sat in a chair near the door, but her husband asked me to sit closer. I told him I wanted him to have that spot, and I was okay seated near the door. He wouldn't accept my offer, so I sat near her bedside. He appeared to be nervous about the surgery. I asked if he was okay and assured him everything would be fine. He nodded his head and told us he was going to the vending machine to get a Coke.

Oh Lord, have mercy! Why did he leave me alone with her? She reached for my hand and told me how sorry she was for breaking off the relationship. My friend said she didn't realize how much she loved me and had been miserable without me. She said she would tell her husband to request orders that would allow them to stay in the area. They had already discussed it, and he gave her the option of choosing their next destination. My emotions and my soul were trying to get the best of me. I gently pulled away and told her she would be alright without me.

After her husband returned, I said a prayer before the nurse took her away. I sat and talked with her husband for about an hour. Finally, the doctor came and gave us a good report, and all was well. I waited for her to wake, making sure she was okay. Her husband and I breathed a sigh of relief when she began to talk. There were no complications with the surgery, so she went home the same day.

Her godfather arrived three days later, just as her husband was leaving for duty. She wanted me to meet him after her pain management got better, and walking was on her list of orders from the doctor. After a few days, she arranged a lunch date for us. Unfortunately, she overdid it that day and soon needed to go back home to rest. She asked me to take her home while leaving her car with her godfather. He offered me gas to take her home, but I declined his offer and agreed to drive my friend back home and make sure she was okay. I asked her if she needed me to find a wheelchair for her so that she wouldn't have to walk far to the car. She told me she would be alright, and we slowly and carefully walked back to the car.

The ride home was quiet, but just before we arrived at the house, she began to tell me that she'd made a mistake by ending our relationship. I didn't respond for fear of saying the wrong thing. I helped her in the house and up the stairs to her bedroom. She hugged me and said, "I'm sorry! I love you! Please don't leave me!"

I responded by telling her that God had ordered her to end our relationship. I told her I loved her too, but I was fighting for my life, and I couldn't stay. I locked her front door, stepped out into the early evening sun, and went to sit in my car for a few minutes. The day's heat encouraged me to finally start my car's engine and back out of her driveway. Although I was hurting, I thanked God for helping me close that door. My heart ached, and I couldn't stop the tears, but I never saw her again from that day forward.

Chapter 7

Chapter 7
A Miracle

The White Family Reunion 2000 was just around the corner. Mom, our extended family, and I had worked hard to put together what we believed would be a successful and memorable event. We began to secure the venue and select the program participants for our scheduled banquet in December 1999. We hadn't hosted a family reunion since 1987, which had been on a much smaller scale. Most of the attendees of that reunion had been the Austin White descendants. This time, the descendants of the two brothers, Austin and Hiram White, would celebrate their heritage together.

We scheduled a four-event gathering, starting with the Thursday evening Meet and Greet. The hotel was gracious, and Mom and I received complimentary accommodations in one of their large suites to show their appreciation for choosing their venue as host for such a sizable event. That was a blessing and a sign that God's hand was upon our planned family gathering. The room was spacious and included an open area for seating. The kitchen was near the dining area, which worked well to set up stations for appetizers. We could tell by the registrations that most of our family would arrive Friday. But for those who traveled Thursday, we prepared appetizers and gave them their family reunion t-shirts from our complimentary suite.

When I started designing the program, I saw Dad's vision on the front page, welcoming and thanking his family for coming to the reunion. The wording included scriptures validating the gathering. Although he was not physically with us to celebrate our family, Mom, the local family, and I would carry out his vision to see his family united as The White Family Reunion. Sharing the idea with Mom was a special moment, and we both shed tears of sorrow and joy at the same time. It was important for Dad to have his family united under the names of Austin and Hiram White.

There was excitement in the air. Many had traveled from several states to attend the reunion. We were nervous, but we also knew God was with us. Thursday's Meet and Greet turned out better than anticipated, and quite a few showed up. The reunion officially started at the Friday night banquet. The Saturday pool picnic was exciting, and Sunday, we set aside to fellowship at our church for the final gathering and the reunion's official close. That Thursday night came and went, and when it was over, Mom and I fell in our beds like two tree trunks. Getting through the first night gave us the confidence to believe everything would be alright.

The banquet consisted of singing, acknowledgments, good food, and words of wisdom. My community choir friends, and my Father in the Lord provided the music. The singing was so good, and my family forgot we were in a restaurant. Even though the room had a divider, the sound of clapping hands and shouts of hallelujah praise filled the entire restaurant. I was afraid the manager would ask us to be quieter and more respectful of the other guest. To my surprise, he said it sounded great, and it was free entertainment for the other guest. There were no complaints.

We Honored my dad's vision of bringing his family together as the White Family reunion. Most of the attendees we had become acquainted with at other reunions.

The presence of God did not let us down, and it showed up as if we were in the church during a revival. Watching some of my family members lifting their hands in praise and others shedding tears answered the question as to why we had to finish what Dad started. It was evident that God wanted to meet my family at this gathering. I knew it was a family reunion, but it was an appointed time for God to bless us. I served as the facilitator, and it was quite a job to try to remain calm while the spirit of the Lord was moving.

I scheduled the acknowledgments before the words from my uncle, the guest speaker. I wanted nothing to interrupt the anointing flow after the words of wisdom to our family. I had also requested an altar call for anyone who would like a chance to receive salvation. My uncle did not disappoint us with his word to his family. During the altar call, my cousin, who I had just become reacquainted with, came to give her life to the Lord. Mom began to lift her hands and walk across the floor, thanking God with undignified praise. I rejoiced and cried, giving thanks to God for orchestrating the entire reunion. The truth is, I believe she came to Christ that night because she knew us, and that made her more comfortable in the familiarity of family. We all hugged her after her confession. Memories that would last forever were made that night.

"So I can guarantee that God's angels are happy about one person who turns to God and changes the way he thinks and acts" Luke 15:10 (GW).

The next day at the picnic, my cousin said she knew something was unique about the reunion. She explained that she was a chain smoker but had not had the urge to smoke since she had arrived that Friday morning. God was working supernaturally at the reunion, and I was mesmerized by His sovereignty and the way He showed Himself to my family.

One of the best things about the reunion was always the food. The Saturday picnic was famous for its over-abundance and wide selection of food. This year's picnic was no different. Mom and I made sure there would be more than enough for everybody. The large all-beef hot dogs, baked beans, macaroni salad and the enormous hamburgers were a definite hit. The dessert was on point! The apple cobbler, peach cobbler, and ice cream were also crowd-pleasers. We couldn't have cooked a better hamburger if we tried. Despite the rain, we danced, played cards, and got to know each other better. God knew it would rain, so He placed in our hearts to have a picnic catered at the hotel.

The children played in the pool, stopped to eat multiple times, and then resumed their wild water games. The adults matched their excitement when the sound of music filled the air. There is no family reunion if you don't get to sway to the O'Jays, Frankie Beverly, and Earth Wind and Fire sounds. Even the children got out of the pool and joined us as we gyrated and maneuvered through the Electric Slide with water dripping from their swimsuits and hair. Even the elderly took their turn shimming down the Soul Train line. We clapped and cheered each other on, laughing and remarking about how surprised we were that some of us still had dance moves.

Among the attendees was a cousin who also loved her family deeply. She and her daughter started bringing the

133

Austin and Hiram descendants together for a family reunion in nineteen eighty-nine. She had eagerly agreed to honor Dad's request to rename the family event to the 'White Family Reunion' gathering. It was an honor to host our family reunion to carry on Dad's legacy of loving his family. The reunion closed out at our home church that Sunday morning. God met us again, and everyone had a great time. After the service, we met in the church parking lot to say our goodbyes. We hugged and kissed as many family members as we could, prayed the Lord's traveling grace and mercy over them, and watched most of them drive out of the church parking lot before we got in our car to go home. Mom and I didn't have enough praise to give our God for His faithfulness to our family. I was thrilled that I'd taken a week off after the reunion. We were both tired and desperately needed a week of recovery time.

Mom and I were sitting in her den a month later, watching The Price Is Right. Whenever I spent the weekday mornings with her, I knew the scheduled lineup: game shows until lunchtime, then a couple of soap operas until late afternoon. Mom and I would scream at the contestants on the gameshows just as if they could hear us. Based on the cheers and screams coming from the den, you would have thought we had won the prizes ourselves. We rolled in imaginary dough by midday, took exotic vacations, and drove luxury cars and campers.

After lunch that day, the phone rang. I scrambled up from the recliner, looking back at the television. I didn't want to miss anything that was happening on the screen. When I answered the phone, the tone in my uncle's voice drew my attention away from the melodrama on the TV. My dad's brother wasn't his usual jolly self. I asked if everything was alright. He began to share the news that our cousin, who received salvation at the reunion, had passed away. She decided against telling us about her condition while at the gathering. So, her death came as a total surprise to the family. She had been diagnosed with terminal cancer, and evidently, she was in the final stages of her illness when she attended the reunion.

I believe she wanted to be with the family she loved before ultimately leaving this world, and she didn't want us to worry about the possibility of her death. My heart was sad to hear of her passing, and she was one person I had planned to get to know better. But on the flip side, I was grateful to God we had said yes to hosting the reunion so she could come and give her heart to Jesus. I hung up the phone and shared the news with Mom. She was also grateful for the opportunity to offer Jesus to my cousin in the pardon of her sins. The information knocked the air out of us. We spent the rest of the evening reminiscing about my cousin and the family reunion.

With a heavy heart, we traveled to her funeral. She had never married, and she had one child. As I thought about it, I grieved that we didn't have a chance to be with her, and she faced death by herself. But God comforted me by saying, *"She was not alone; the angels escorted her into my presence."*

Once we were comfortably seated at the funeral, I noticed that the program offered a chance to share reflections. I took the opportunity to share what happened at the reunion for those who didn't attend and may not have known that she had given her life to Christ. I wanted to ease the minds of our family while expressing the love of God for our cousin. God had a plan to save our cousin's soul, and we

135

were unaware of it. We understood the mind of God when we saw her accept Jesus. I was stunned by how God arranged for my cousin to have a chance to choose Him, and he orchestrated it before her demise. Once again, it showed the loving-kindness of the God we serve. We all left that day, resting in the knowledge that God is more sovereign than we could ever imagine, and He's more thoughtful than we could ever be.

I continued to assist Mom with Women's Sunday and serve my Father in the Lord, the senior pastor. He kept me encouraged while I was healing from my last personal failure. I never discussed my decision to go back to my old lifestyle, but he was also prophetic. So, I'm sure he knew I was struggling, and he was praying for deliverance. Every Sunday became a breath of fresh air for me. The residue of my past relationship no longer gripped me.

A couple of months later, my pastor received an invitation to share the word of the Lord with a nearby congregation. I've always believed in serving in whatever capacity needed, and God gave unknown blessings to individuals who served leaders. Some have confused the idea of true servanthood with idol worship. We have a biblical example of servanthood when reading about Moses and Joshua and Elijah and Elisha. These scripture-based stories give us confirmation that servanthood is of God.

I picked up my Spiritual Father on a beautiful Sunday evening. I anticipated a great time together, making our way to the hosting church. He had already taught me many lessons, and he always had something funny to say. I never left his presence without feeling loved and empowered.

While I was driving, a prophetic word came through my Father in the Lord. The power of this word almost caused me to pull the car over. We had been laughing and talking non-stop since he had gotten in my car. Suddenly, he became reflective and quiet. I gave a glance over at him. I could tell that he was deep in thought, so I decided to give him the remainder of our time together in the car to himself. Thinking that he was preparing himself for the message he would deliver once we arrived at the church and did not want to distract him, I kept my eyes on the road.

A few miles later, he broke the silence in the car. Without even turning his face toward me, he said, ***"The Lord has called you to be a pastor, and you will know when the timing is right to obey."***

I was devastated by his words. It took me a moment to process that he was speaking to me. In an attempt to downplay the seriousness and the awkwardness of the moment, I jokingly said, "I wouldn't pastor ten roaches with an extra-strength can of Raid!" Suddenly nervous, I laughed uncontrollably at the thought. He thought my joke was pretty funny too, and I was relieved to see him throw his head back and laugh with me. But the laughter didn't last long. He stood firm on the Lord's word, and again he expressed that the Lord would reveal the timing.

My heart sank. I knew this was not going away. I couldn't deny my pastor was prophetic, and if he said it, I knew God had spoken it. My heart constantly desired to remain with him, doing ministry, and he was so faithful in his desire to see me restored. How could I leave this man who had taken on considerable criticism for allowing this backslidden preacher to play music in the house of God?

We arrived at the church, and I couldn't concentrate on anything during the service. My mind was absorbed with thoughts about what my future would look like as a pastor. The word spoken over me took me through a mind-boggling dilemma. Growing up in the church and seeing firsthand how church politics can get, I had developed an unfavorable view of pastoring.

I couldn't understand why anyone in their right mind would want that job. For some, it may be the ultimate position in life. The thought as to why God would even call me after all my challenges baffled me. Who would want me to be their pastor? Where would I pastor, and what would be the church's name? The last twelve months of my life had been like walking through a maze. My confidence stalled, and I found myself overthinking things that would have generally come as second nature before my fall. How could I possibly lead anybody when I was unsure of my steps? I spent the entire service creating a mental list of questions and excuses. Like Moses, when the Lord came to me, I needed to prepare my argument.

The ride back from the church was a relatively quiet one. My pastor had expended a lot of energy during the service, so he used the ride home as a chance to replenish and regroup. I was grateful for the silence. I dropped him off at his house, wished him a peaceful night's rest, and headed to Mom's house to check on her.

I walked into Mom's house, and she was excited to hear about the service. I explained what I remembered, and I tried to be excited to tell her about it. She saw straight through me, and before long, she asked if I was alright. I played it off by explaining that I was just tired, but the service had been a blessing. I quickly made sure Mom had everything she needed, and I walked home to get ready for Monday.

I couldn't wait to have some time alone. I felt like I needed a pow-wow with God. I had some questions to ask, and I needed a chance to state my case. Here I was, coming out of grieving for my dad and still broken-hearted over a relationship that wasn't good for me. What was it that God saw in me that I didn't see? I refused to share it with Mom because I knew she would have agreed with God's word for my life. I even asked my Father in the Lord to keep that word to himself. I didn't want anybody to know the prophecy, and I was already under enough pressure. He agreed not to discuss the word of wisdom with anybody.

My life had just started to feel as if it was back on track. The pain of the last relationship had somewhat healed, and there were no more nights of crying. I'd forgiven myself and was moving forward. Seeking the Lord's presence was once again becoming my usual practice. Now and then, I'd hear the words spoken by my Father in the Lord that Sunday evening. In my heart, I didn't want to appear not receptive to the concept of the Lord. My faith was less than a mustard seed, and I saw no possible way for me to become anybody's pastor. On the other hand, there is never a choice to obey God. Even if I didn't see it happening, it wouldn't keep God from performing this miracle and having His way.

After a few minutes alone with God, I decided to return to Mom's house and prepare for the workweek. She was well, and her dog, Crystal, laid by her side, watching me settle in. After my shower, I was ready to jump into bed. It wasn't going to be any staring at the ceiling for me; sleep was calling my name.

That night, God chose to visit me while I was asleep. The scene He showed me involved my position at work. I had been the jewelry manager for three years. But, in this vision, I resigned from my full-time job and started working part-time. God told me to register for a barber school in January. He also told me Mom would help finance this career change. I woke up thinking what in the world was all that! Although I would cut the hair of some of the community choir boys, my uncles, and my dad in years past, I was not ready for this new adjustment.

"15 in dreams, in visions of the night when deep sleep falls on men as they lie on their beds" Job 33:15 (TLB).

Eventually, I enrolled in classes at our Community College. I'd worked in five different departments and managed three at work, trying to figure out which one would be best suited for on a part-time basis. I visited the college on my days off and spoke to the Health and Beauty department administrator, and I collected all the information about classes and tuition costs. He explained that they didn't have a barber school, but I could learn to cut hair at the cosmetology school.

There were only three months until the start of the course, and I would need time to begin transitioning to my new schedule in early January. Eventually, I built up the courage to share what God had shown me with Mom. I never explained that she agreed to help finance my coursework in the vision. But before I could finish discussing resigning from my management position, Mom volunteered to help me financially. I reached over and kissed and hugged her neck. What a weight off my shoulders! She had enough confidence

140

to invest in me financially and that gave me the push I needed.

I couldn't wait to show Mom all the information the college had given me. It appeared everything was working out for me. Now, I only needed to speak with my manager and give her my plans for January 1st. I scheduled a meeting with her, and it went well. She was happy for me, but she did tell me that she would miss having me in management. I appreciated her support of my efforts to do something different. I had managed departments for twelve years, and now my responsibilities were gone.

Before I knew it, it was time for my first day of class. I took that entire week off from work to adjust to school. My courses started at 8 a.m. The night before, my first class was challenging. I tossed and turned because I was so nervous. I didn't know what to expect. I prayed that I'd pass the course and the state exam. Then, it occurred that this was God's idea, and He planned for me to be successful. All I had to do was to walk according to His will.

Before I knew it, a week had gone by, and we'd met all the teachers. The following Monday was a holiday. We resumed our classes that Tuesday and the deadline ended for new students to register. Around 10 a.m., the instructor walked in with a student. He introduced her by saying her name and saying he didn't know why he allowed her to register beyond the deadline. Sensing the awkwardness of the moment and the new student's uneasiness, the instructor jokingly threw in that he had only accepted her late registration because she was cute. We all laughed, and immediately the tension on the new student's face disappeared.

The teacher asked me to show the new student the daily routine. I showed her around the department and explained the daily routine to her. I made sure she understood that the program was strict about time management and that we were practicing as if we were in a salon. She needed to know that the course would be grading her on her ability to clock in and out on time and that she would only have thirty minutes for lunch. It seemed so restrictive, but I informed her that sometimes the thirty-minute lunch was doable, and sometimes we didn't make it. She relaxed when I told her that I would take full responsibility for being late. Occasionally, my appetite called for fried chicken or a double hamburger, which meant leaving the campus. Later, I realized that she ate wholesome clean meals like Brussel sprouts and fruit.

While riding with my Brussel sprout-eating classmate to lunch one day, I discovered that she could sing well. She was kind enough to record herself singing Happy Birthday to my mom as a gift on her special day. Mom loved the recording, and she wanted to meet the young lady with a beautiful voice. Mom eventually met her, and together we convinced her to come with us to church and join our community choir.

During class and on our lunch breaks, we often talked about owning a salon and a Christian café. We both agreed that the atmosphere in most salons and barbershops was usually filled with gossip and drama. Our goal was to provide an excellent barber experience in an amazingly uplifting atmosphere. We decided to go into business together after graduation and state board exams. She had been barbering for years before enrolling in school, so all she needed was her

142

license. On the other hand, I needed more training to raise my cutting skills to industry standards.

November came, and we were all very excited. We achieved our goals and passed the required exams for graduation. It was an incredible accomplishment to walk across the stage and receive an Associate of Arts Degree. Thirteen months before that time, I had no idea how to complete God's instructions. With His help, I finished school and prepared for the state exam before the holidays.

Thanksgiving was always a time of celebration with my family. Mom asked if I would drive her to the Homecoming festivities at her Alma Mata. Since her college days, she hadn't attended any of the gatherings of the annual Homecoming festivals. In disbelief, I wondered why. The answer she gave me was shocking! Bashfully, she explained how Daddy was always afraid an old boyfriend of hers might show up for homecoming, so he never wanted her to participate. I just stood still in disbelief for a minute, shaking my head, thinking of all the girlfriends he had while they were married. Mom quickly saw my expression; she knew exactly what I was thinking. She never wanted me to think negatively about my dad, so she quickly said, "Girl, I'm free now! Let's go and have a great time!" I chuckled at her girlish enthusiasm and started packing our things. We had a marvelous time traveling to our destination. Seeing Mom smile and enjoy her friends from college made me feel good.

It had been almost two years since Dad's death, and we had adjusted well. Mom had been such a great supporter while I attended school during the day and worked part-time at night. She was driving herself to all her favorite shops and doctor's visits. I was so proud that she pressed herself to remain independent even though her whole body was aching from fibromyalgia. Caring for Mom was a priority, and I promised Dad to see her face every day and assist her in any way possible. Knowing that she was cared for, happy, and wanting nothing gave me great peace of mind.

December was here, and it was time to walk across the stage in our cap and gown. Mom and my classmate's families screamed at the top of their lungs as they called our names and handed us our diplomas. I breathed a big sigh of relief. Now we needed to study and prepare for the state exam.

Late in January, Mom would travel about two hours with some of her friends to a women's conference. I didn't worry about her going without me because I knew she was in good hands. Her friends would ensure she ate, took her medicine, and assisted her while walking with a cane. After a long day at the conference, they arrived home, and it was dark when they dropped her off. She was tired but excited and ready to share how blessed she was by the gathering. I was encouraged by her excitement. Once again, It was a sign that Mom was adapting well to her life without Dad. She showed me that she had no plans to linger at home, depressed and lonely.

We attended church the next day and had dinner together afterward. Once we arrived home, I began to help Mom undress. I reached out to help her take off her jacket, and suddenly, she began to scream and hold her chest. I had no idea what was happening, but I could tell that she was in distress. I did the only thing I could think to do. While calling on Jesus, I got Mom to lay down on the bed while I loosened her clothes and dialed 911. As I talked to the 911 dispatcher, Mom rolled from side to side on the bed in terrible pain. Thank God we lived near the fire station and the emergency responders were there in less than five minutes.

The paramedics skillfully worked on Mom. Once they got her to relax, checked her vitals, and placed an oxygen mask over her mouth, she showed signs that the excruciating pain she had been in was subsiding. When they finally had her stable, the paramedic told me that they would be transporting her to the hospital. Unofficially, he explained that it seemed likely that she had had a heart attack.

My heart was racing. I was trying my best to think clearly, but I was terrified. I quickly called my dad's sister and asked if she would go with me to the hospital. She loved Mom just as if she were her blood sister, which was a blessing for me. I knew I could always depend on her for help. By the time I ran back to the house, grabbing my purse and keys, she was there to pick me up. I told her I would drive, so she got out of her car and got in on the passenger side of my car. She understood that I was too nervous about riding along while driving the speed limit and stopping at every light, and I could get us there in half the time.

We made it to the ER, and they had already taken Mom back for tests. The triage nurse escorted my aunt and me back to a small room. They told us the doctor would be in to talk to us as soon as they could get Mom settled and get some answers. After about an hour, the doctor came in and confirmed that Mom had had a heart attack. He walked us to a hospital room on the cardiac floor. I was relieved to see Mom resting quietly there in a hospital bed. She was still on oxygen, but she didn't seem to be in any pain. The doctor explained to Mom and me that she had a blockage, which meant she needed a double-bypass. It wasn't what I wanted to hear, but I was very thankful that God had spared her life.

As soon as I got home, I started contacting my family, telling them about Mom's condition and asking for prayers. I tried my best not to think the worst. Dad had been pretty healthy his entire life, and we never expected he would die before Mom. But she had survived, and he was no longer with us.

I contacted my job and arranged to use my sick time and personal leave time to be with Mom until she recovered. It had been two years since Dad's death, but it still felt very fresh, emotionally. After an extended stay at the hospital, I made it home. I sat down in Mom's chair, holding her dog, Crystal. I began to talk to God while gently petting the dog's head. Somehow, petting and comforting the family dog and pouring my heart to God in prayer brought me peace. Once again, I knew I needed to be steadfast in my faith for Mom, exemplifying courage, and assurance in God.

I met with the cardiologist the following day to discuss Mom's double bypass surgery plans. He informed us that the veins in Mom's legs weren't in good enough condition for the operation, and he suggested using the veins in her arms to do the procedure as an alternative. We listened attentively as the doctor gave us the possible outcomes after a patient had had a double bypass. He explained that most patients recovered well, and their mobility increased, allowing them to walk better and exercise freely. After much prayer, Mom and I agreed that this was our best option. We both wanted her to enjoy life as much as possible without any restrictions.

Mom's primary physician had prescribed several different medications for her, and Coumadin, a blood thinner used to prevent clotting and strokes, was part of her daily prescription regimen. The cardiologist told us that she would need to stop taking the Coumadin for five days so her blood would have time to thicken for the operation. My faithful aunt hung in there with me during the mornings when the doctor made his morning rounds. It was good to have her there. She remembered what I had forgotten, and she asked the questions I couldn't think to ask. I appreciated her level-headedness and her unwavering support during that time.

I spent the morning and lunchtime with Mom every day, and I would take a nap after they served her lunch and then return to sit with her again by 5:00 pm. Mom needed to know she was not alone and that I was her support, and she already knew that I loved her. She had seen many sicknesses, but this was the most severe diagnosis.

By that Thursday, her blood was showing signs of thickening. That was the excellent report we were waiting to hear, and it meant the heart surgeon could finalize arrangements to schedule her surgery.

Mom was full of joy even though she faced a season of uncertainty in her life. There was a chance that she would not survive a double bypass, but one thing was for sure. Either way, it went; she was confident in her knowledge that her Father had a plan, and it would be best for her life. It helped me to witness her strong faith in action all over again. Through the years, her example of endless love and constant faith in God molded me and convinced me to make Him my God.

I also felt better knowing that the county's top cardiac surgical team would be handling Mom's case. My faith was in God, who would guide the surgeon's hands as he repaired the damage to Mom's heart. The enemy tried to counsel me by saying, "You prayed for your dad's life, and God didn't answer!" I must admit it seemed as if he had a valid point. But I understood God is never a failure, even if He doesn't give you what you prayed.

It was the eve of the surgery, and I had contacted family and friends to give the procedure's specific time. I requested they all call Mom's name in prayer during the exact time the surgery would begin. I spent time with her in the surgical waiting room before the staff rolled her bed through the automatic doors. I prayed with her, kissed her, and promised her that I would be waiting there to see her when she woke up. Although she would be heavily sedated and unable to talk, I needed to declare she would see me again. I wanted that to be the last words she heard before the anesthesiologist put her to sleep.

My business partner and friend, who had become a second daughter to Mom, agreed to be with me while the operation took place. I so appreciated her love and concern for my family. I was nervous, and with no blood siblings, I needed her support, and it brought comfort waiting for the completion of a six-hour surgery. She somehow knew exactly when to talk to me and when to let me sit quietly with my thoughts. In between prayers, we made tentative plans for the upcoming salon.

After about an hour, a surgeon came out to update us on Mom's progress. I held my breath as he approached us. I didn't know what he was going to say. I silently prayed, "Oh my God, please don't let him say something unexpected went wrong, and we lost Mrs. White." I watched him walk towards us, it seemed as if he was walking in slow motion, but I kept my eyes on him with each step, but at the same time, my whole body froze with fear.

He smiled and asked, "Are you Kamia?"

"Yes, Sir," My voice sounded faint, barely above a whisper. His smile was warm, and some of my fears and tension left my body. He started by saying the procedure was going well, and they would probably be able to complete the double bypass in five more hours. I breathed a sigh of relief, thanked him for the update, and settled back into the less than comfortable waiting-room chair, taking a short catnap.

Another three hours passed, and the surgeon came out again to speak with me. I looked for a smile and that tale-tell pep in his step to help me determine if this would be good news or bad news. This time he said they had run into a minor complication. He explained that using the veins in my mom's arm instead of in her legs was more complicated, and it would extend the time of her surgery. Before I could panic, he moved on to say that the good news was that the veins in her arms were strong enough to be used as a substitute for the damaged artery. I was so happy; I jumped up from my seat and hugged him. I thanked him as I patted his back. He laughed and told me he still had some work to do, so I needed to release my grip on him and allow him to get back to his patient. I turned him loose and loudly thanked God for working everything out for me.

After hearing that good news, my friend convinced me to go with her to the hospital cafeteria to eat lunch. My appetite was nonexistent up that point, and my thoughts and prayers had taken all my attention. But now that I had allowed myself to breathe, I noticed an empty feeling in my belly. There were many choices, but I chose something light to eat that would help me stay alert. The cafeteria had long lines, so my friend ordered our food, and I walked outside to get some fresh air and thank God for His goodness. I also made a few phone calls to update family and friends.

By the time I had finished picking at the food my friend had chosen for me, Mom had been in surgery for six hours, and they were still working on her. I tried to keep my thoughts upbeat. But as the hour hand on the wall clock got closer to indicating that we were approaching the seventh hour, I could feel my stress level increasing. Other families had loved ones in surgery simultaneously as Mom's surgery, but they had already received good news and were no longer there. We were the only family members waiting to get confirmation that our loved one's operation had been a success.

Another hour passed, and the surgeon walked into the cardiac surgery waiting room again. He smiled and duplicated the pep in his step from the last visit. He looked to be at ease. The operation had been a success, and Mom was in ICU. It was customary for bypass patients to receive twenty-four-hour care after surgery, and they needed constant monitoring. After forty-five minutes, they allowed us to see her.

I tried to remember the videos shown to me before Mom's surgery. Viewing the videos would help me process Mom's recovery time and help me stay calm when it was time to visit her right after surgery. As we approached Mom's room hallway, I whispered to my friend, asking what that noise was and where it was coming from, and could it be in her room. It sounded as if it was coming from the direction we were heading, and the noise was a loud swooshing sound.

Although I appreciated the consultations and videos, nothing could have prepared me for what I saw when entering her ICU room. The nurse taking care of Mom saw the fear and shock on my face, and it wasn't long before tears were rolling down my cheeks. Mom's body was swollen beyond recognition. How did that happen? The nurse quickly explained that the swelling was normal. She calmed me by saying every bypass patient has gone through fluid removal. She pointed to a machine that was about four feet tall. The machine's function was like a vacuum, sucking the excess liquid from my mom's unconscious body. Once the device fills, it would be taken away and replaced by another machine, repeating the process. The nurse informed us that Mom would be in the ICU while extracting the liquid and waiting for her blood pressure to return within the normal range.

After the initial shock, I gradually walked closer to Mom's bedside. I just wanted to touch her, even if she wasn't aware I was there. She was intubated, sedated, and so bloated and swollen. It was hard to believe that this was a regular part of the recovery process. I began to speak to her the word of God through faith, knowing that it was crucial to her progress and my walk of faith.

"The Lord has brought you through the surgery, and you will not die; instead, you will live and tell what the Lord has done" Psalm 118:17 (GW).

Ten days passed, and Mom was looking better. There were no more intubation tubes, and the loud-sounding equipment was gone. They moved her to the cardiac floor for approximately ten more days. Mom's pre-existing conditions justified additional caution and a slower recovery. She had diabetes and high blood pressure for years. Although she missed having her freedom and being at home, she understood the measures to prevent any medical setbacks. Mom felt much better, and she was thankful for the cardiac specialist who had handled her case.

Her recovery was going well, and rehab was the next destination. Again, this was part of the plan to ensure all bypass patients return to a healthy life. There was one complication that bothered Mom. She couldn't lay down flat on her back and continue to breathe. She described it as feeling like her lungs stopped responding while lying flat. At first, the nurses didn't believe that was happening. Some said they had never had that experience with any other cardiac patients. I understood they had never witnessed this complication in their patients before, but Mom was experiencing a great deal of discomfort so that she would not lay down. She insisted on sleeping in an upright position.

The doctor visited with Mom and checked on her progress. He released her discharge papers and admitted her to the rehab facility. I addressed my concerns with him about Mom's inability to breathe while lying flat. He gave the most concrete answer to the issue Mom had. He explained that a small percentage of patients' lung muscles go to sleep during surgery, and it happens when the surgeon inadvertently touches the lung tissue during the procedure. I much appreciated the doctor addressing my concerns. He gave us hope and said it was a temporary condition, and Mom would soon recover fully from her discomfort.

I transported her to a rehab located in a nearby city. I hoped she would be closer, but her insurance recommended this rehab because of their excellent reputation. That was all I needed to know. I wanted the absolute best and safest care for mom while she recovered. I adjusted my schedule to see her every day, hearing my dad's voice reminding me of my responsibility toward her. There was only one problem; my job required that each manager close the store one night out of the week. My schedule started at noon on the day I closed and ended at nine, making it hard for me to travel to see her. Thank God for my friend! She volunteered to visit Mom and check on her when I couldn't make it. Mom was excited and grateful for the help her adopted daughter gave our family.

Mom settled in and began to adjust to her new schedule. She had deep wounds on her arms from bypass surgery. Every day, a nurse came to clean, pack, and bandage her wounds. There were days that her arms showed signs of struggling to heal and close; sometimes, the scars would reopen during the night. Diabetes caused the healing process to slow down dramatically.

The rehab staff was courteous and very attentive to Mom and her needs. Every day she spent time in the gym doing chair exercises in her room. The goal was to help her live as independently as possible. During the evening, my friend would meet me at rehab to prop Mom's head up with pillows so she could sleep at night.

One day the nurse asked if I had a small dog I could bring to Mom. I agreed to get Crystal the next day. Mom's interaction with her dog gave her another incentive to do well during her therapy sessions. Crystal was so happy to see her mom. It had been almost a month since Mom had held her baby, so they were both smiling from ear to ear when I finally brought Crystal.

Mom was so considerate. She wanted me to stay at home and rest every other day. There was no way I was going to do that. I came every day except for the days I closed. It hurt not to see Mom every day. I missed and loved her so much. Somehow, I felt Dad knew I was doing my best. My aunt called Mom every day, as well. We all did our best.

Finally, it was time for Mom's release from rehab. What an exciting day that was! My friend met me at the facility, and together we packed Mom's belongings. While ensuring we had everything, Mom noticed her special cardiac teddy bear was underneath her bed covers. The hospital gave all bypass patients the same cute little teddy bear to help them cough. I double-checked under the bed to make sure we had everything. I didn't want to come back for anything.

The nurse brought a wheelchair to help us get Mom to the car. We thanked them for the care they had given her. We started a hugging party, and even a few of the nurses who had grown attached to Mom shed a few tears. Even though she had only been with them for three weeks, Mom obviously had an enormous impact on some of them. That was understandable; Mom was so loving and easy to care for. I knew she hadn't given them any trouble. It was a bittersweet moment for me. I was happy to be taking Mom home, and on the other hand, I was a little fearful. I reminded myself that God was with me, and He would strengthen me to be Mom's caregiver until she was healthy again.

The next day, the nurse came to the house to dress Mom's wounds and take her blood pressure. She could see the concern in Mom's eyes. The scars on her arms didn't seem to heal as fast as we thought they should. The nurse took a close look at them and assured us that, in time, they would recover.

The cardiac surgeon scheduled an appointment the next week to evaluate Mom's progress. I took her to the doctor's office in a wheelchair, bringing an oxygen tank. Her specialist was excited to see how well Mom looked. It had been two months since he had last seen her. The doctor checked her blood pressure and was pleased with the reading. He asked Mom if she was able to lay down flat to sleep. Unfortunately, she informed him that she still couldn't sleep in a reclined position, indicating that her lungs had not responded yet. So, sleeping sitting up in her recliner was her only choice. He didn't seem alarmed by her answer. He just made a quick note on her chart and assured her that the lung muscles would function again.

Every week, Mom continued to get better. Her reliance on oxygen decreased, and she felt good enough to start cooking light meals. Since we had a gas stove, Mom couldn't use the oxygen near it, and I was afraid she would forget. So, as a reminder, I posted a sign on the wall in big black letters. The sign read NO OXYGEN PAST THIS POINT, and I posted it at her eye level on the wall just before she entered the kitchen. While at work, I would call her around eight-thirty every morning to make sure she had breakfast before her nurse arrived to dress her wounds and take her vitals. I'd call back at noon to get a report from the nurse's visit and make sure she'd eaten the lunch I prepared for her and left in the refrigerator. We had a routine, and it helped me not worry so much while I was away from her.

Chapter 8

Chapter 8
Where Do I Go From Here

It had been six months since the surgery, and Mom was on a steady path to recovery. Although her road to a full recovery was longer than I wanted it to be, her cardiac specialist was confident that she was right on schedule for a healthier and more vibrant life. Knowing that her life was going to be better sealed it for me.

Mom's use of oxygen had decreased quite a bit. The medical equipment facility now brought one large and one small aluminum cylinder per week for Mom's use. She was no longer using the oxygen around the house, and we both had relaxed our constant vigil of checking and double-checking the gauge, which indicated the level of oxygen remaining in the tanks. Her lungs were getting stronger every day, and that tight grip of anxiousness was slowly loosening its grip.

One day Mom and I decided to go to Red Lobster for dinner. The lure of their famous cheddar bay biscuits overrode our earlier declaration that we would spend the whole day in our pajamas. We quickly dressed, and on the way out the door, I grabbed a cylinder of oxygen for Mom to use while dining. The tank always made a hissing noise while in operation, but it wasn't loud enough to be bothersome. Mom and I had grown so accustomed to its sound; it just blended in with the other hisses and hums in the house. Once inside the restaurant, that familiar noise blended in and became part of the usual symphony of sounds associated with people enjoying companionship and good food. Like everyone else in the restaurant, we laughed, discussed recent events, and enjoyed our food.

Suddenly, I realized the cylinder wasn't making any noise, and its contribution to the concert had ended, which meant it was out of commission. Oh, Lord! I instantly remembered I didn't check the oxygen level of the cylinder before Mom and I rushed out the door. Immediately, I began to panic on the inside! How could I be so careless! How did I forget to make sure Mom's oxygen would last the entire time we were out for dinner? I forced myself to appear calm on the outside, and for the next five minutes, I secretly observed Mom as she talked, laughed at her jokes, and enjoyed her meal. My hidden anxiety lessened as I realized that she wasn't aware there was no oxygen in her tank.

With great relief, I heard the Lord say, *"I have healed her, and she no longer needs the oxygen."* He instructed me to ask Mom how well she was breathing before telling her she was without oxygen. I wanted to sound confident so that she wouldn't freak out and hyper-ventilate. She had depended on the oxygen for seven months and finding out that she suddenly was on her own might be too much for her. At that moment, I was even having trouble breathing, and I didn't have any respiratory issues!

I began to pray in my heart calmly, asking God to help Mom not to fear. When the time was right, I started by asking how her breathing was. Without any thought, she said it was great and felt good. I sighed, thinking that was a great start. Next, I told her that God had healed her lungs, which was why her breathing was better than it had ever been.

Mom clapped her hands and shook her head. Yes! So far, so good! I was on a roll. "Mom, you've been breathing on your own for the last hour because healing has taken place. I forgot to check the oxygen level in your cylinder before we left home. It's empty, Mom." I saw fear trying to overtake her as I talked, but I grabbed her hands and said, "Take a deep breath, let it out, and take another deep breath and let it out." When she was finally able to process what I was saying and realized that she was healed and breathing fine on her own, she hugged my neck while praising God. We called the medical equipment company the following Monday to pick up the remaining oxygen cylinders.

The Lord was touching Mom's body and making her completely whole. Her walking distance had increased, she was mobile without a cane, her lung had healed, and she could lie flat on her back while sleeping. I was so excited to see her slimming down and moving on with life. I still called every morning during my first break and then again during my lunch break. After work, I checked on her first. Doing that allowed me to keep the promise I had made to Dad, and it put my mind at peace while I was away from her.

We had restricted Mom's whereabouts while she was recuperating. Now that she had fully recovered, there was no stopping her. Every Saturday, I started taking her back to her favorite spot, the flea market. She was thrilled to be out and about, but I noticed something different about how she dressed. Even though Mother Nature had the summer temperature set on a hot boil, she wore long sleeves. When I asked her about it, Mom explained that strangers always stared at the scars on her arms. Sometimes, little kids would ask her what happened to her arms, making her uncomfortable. So, she decided it would be best to cover up those old wounds. I felt terrible about the whole thing. I wanted to get with everyone who looked at the scars and the children about the rudeness of asking strangers questions about personal matters. Mom was a trooper, as always, and she simply said, "It's okay, Mamma's Baby." I would have been content just to let it go if I didn't know it bothered her enough to make her change the way she dressed. Since it obviously upset her, it bothered me.

After coming home from a long day at work, Mom had some exciting news for me. She decided to join the aquatic exercise program to reduce her joint pain. I teased her about having to wear a swimsuit. "Bring out that sexy two-piece swimsuit you're hiding," I said. Blushing and almost turning beet red, Mom let me know she would be wearing a one-piece. I laughed so hard because I knew her upbringing made her uncomfortable wearing any kind of bathing suit, even the modest one-piece. She scheduled the aquatics class every Tuesday and Thursday. I knew it would take her going to a couple of those classes before she became comfortable with the thought of being in a bathing suit. But she was determined to make the best of everything.

The aquatic exercise gave her a steady schedule to follow, and she was happy to have something to do. Mondays, Wednesdays, and Fridays were her days to do with as she pleased, and she had no trouble finding ways to occupy her time.

Mom loved her church, and nothing gave her greater pleasure than coming up with different programs and services to improve it and make it more productive. Being on the computer was her passion. She developed a church newsletter, and It was informative and entertaining. She made sure it included birthdays, events, and past sermons topics with related scriptures. Developing and maintaining the newsletter became one of her favorite hobbies.

Mom was now driving herself to the mall, doing light grocery shopping, and visiting her family and friends. I was so proud of her for fighting through and not giving up when things were tough. Her faith had once again taken her through to victory. I continued to call my out-of-town family, giving them regular updates on Mom's health. They, too, were happy she recovered and was better than before.

One weekend I was taking Mom on a short road trip so we both could have a change of scenery. I had gotten up early, prepared breakfast, and went home to get dressed. When I returned to check on Mom, she told me she was ready to go. I noticed, to my surprise, she was dressed in a comfortable short sleeve blouse. She hadn't worn that type of shirt in months, not since she drew so much attention in short sleeve blouses. I casually asked about her outfit. I wanted to make sure she hadn't simply forgotten to put on a long sleeve blouse like she usually wore when we were going out. I didn't want her upset by the stares and questions of the insensitive people we were bound to encounter on our trip. I wanted her to enjoy our little excursion without feeling self-conscientious about the scars on her arms.

Mom sensed my apprehension and my concern for her. She quietly explained that the Lord had a conversation about her insecurities. According to Mom, the *"Lord told her there was no need for her to hide her scars. "They are evidence of your victory," He said. "Even I have scars in Heaven."*

I was speechless, and the Lord began to minister to us, right there in Mom's living room. We had some church, and we almost didn't make it out of the house. Mom welcomed questions about her scars from that day forward, helping others believe in our God's existence and power.

So, the other disciples told him, "We have seen the Lord!" Thomas told them, "I refuse to believe this unless I see the nail marks put my finger into them, and my hand in his side" John 20:25 (GW).

Mom had also started hosting Women's Day once a month at church again. I had previously organized them during her recovery and tried to do what I'd seen her do. It seemed to do well, but I was happy for her to lead on those Sundays. I learned a great deal from Mother White as I watched God use her to usher in His presence. There would be many Sundays that the Lord would overwhelm us, and all we needed was exhortation, an altar call, and no preaching. Whenever she had chosen me to teach, I was happy when the Lord rewrote the program. I was so drawn to the Holy Spirit, having His way never bothered me to let go of the written plan. But this would only happen if Mom scheduled me. The other participants were not willing to give up their teaching opportunities. We ended up staying in church longer than needed. It taught me that the plan of the Holy Spirit was the right plan to follow. I learned that it wasn't that I'd studied in vain, but God was sovereign and could use my sermon anytime.

" When the Holy Spirit, who is truth, comes, he shall guide you into all truth, for he will not be presenting his own ideas, but will be passing on to you what he has heard. He will tell you about the future" John 16:13 (TLB).

One Sunday morning, the Lord said, *"Tell my people to repent!"* I had heard the Lord's voice many times before, so I knew it was Him speaking to me.

There was an entire conversation between God and me in my mind. First, I needed some clarity. "God, you want me to tell the church to repent?" Trying to wrap my head around God's instructions didn't sit right with me. I just didn't feel like I was the best person to deliver that particular message. My track record hadn't exactly been free of missteps, and some of my fellow congregants didn't share the belief that God would use me to that extent. After all my reasoning, God didn't change His mind.

I attempted to abort my mission during the service, and the Holy Spirit had utterly consumed the place, and I didn't budge. I always approached, asking permission to give a corporate prophesy to the church because he was the church's overseer.

" Remember that a person who has a message from God has the power to stop himself or wait his turn. 33 God is not one who likes things to be disorderly and upset. He likes harmony, and he finds it in all the other churches" 1 Corinthians 14: 32-33 (TLB).

After a few minutes, we moved on to the next phase of the service. Boy, I was breathing such a sigh of relief! I thanked God He heard my reasoning and canceled the assignment. Well, not so fast!

Part of my regular duties was to help with receiving the offering. So, as always, I got up and stood behind the offering table and instructed others to come and give. As I stood there, the anointing of God began to take hold of my body. I began to shake and speak in an unknown tongue. In my head, I started saying, 'No God! Please don't make me do it!' The more I resisted, the more my body shook out of control. To the people sitting in the audience, I imagine it must have looked like I was doing the Funky Chicken dance.

Then, I heard my beloved Father in the Lord say, "Sister White, tell us what the Lord is saying." Finally, with his encouragement, I released the word of the Lord to the waiting congregation. A few responded and came to the altar. We repented that we had not walked in love for our brethren, and strife was among us. The weight and difficulty of the assignment, plus the thought of my willingness to abort it, caused tears to flood from my eyes. From that day forward, I understood that my gift belonged to God, He was in control of it, and there was nothing I could do about it.

Emotionally, I was a complete mess! So, Mom offered to drive us home. She was quiet and waited to speak to me when we arrived home. I knew she had been praying that I would be willing and able to complete my assignment. We sat down at our favorite meeting place, the kitchen bar. Mom said, "Baby, I know it's hard to obey God when you feel inadequate. But you must forgive yourself and believe that God has forgiven you." The flood of tears started again. Mom reached over and grabbed my hand. "Thirty-six years ago, you were just a few months old, and the church mothers prophesied that God marked you. You can't outrun the call on your life."

I fell into her arms, sobbing uncontrollably. Getting over people and their opinions would be the most significant victory in my life. Several years before that day, I made the wrong decision because I couldn't handle who I was in God. I allowed the pressure of being surrounded by jealous people to push me in the wrong direction. But now, I refused to take steps backward. I had to pass the test.

Mom gave me the time I needed to get myself together. While I sat at the counter sniffling and wiping tears, she quietly moved about the kitchen, warming the food she had prepared before we left for morning worship service. By the time she had prepared everything, I had gotten myself under control.

Mom cooked butter beans and peas mixed, rice, cornbread, and a mean crockpot roast. Our dessert came from the local Publix grocery store. We were in love with their birthday cakes! So, when we had a craving for cake, one of us would say, 'Whose birthday is it today?' The other would respond with 'I don't know, but it's somebody's birthday, and we're going to celebrate!' We would giggle like two schoolgirls, hiding a secret. We agreed that we just couldn't forget the ice cream; there is no such thing as a party with no ice cream to go on top of the cake.

After we ate and celebrated some unknown person's birthday, we were fuller than two ticks, and there was nothing left to do but take a Sunday nap. Everybody knows that there is no nap like a Sunday nap! They are better than a Monday nap or even a Saturday nap. I can't explain it, but they just are!

Mom relaxed in her recliner while I wobbled over to the couch. I knew this was going to be a good two-hour nap. While I was in a deep sleep, God visited me in a vision. In the image, I saw Mom, heavily pregnant. It looked as if she was a full nine months pregnant, and she was almost ready to deliver her baby. As a result of her unexplained pregnancy,

165

the saints were upset and treated her very harshly. In my vision, I showed up and began to defend Mom. Although I didn't know why she was pregnant, I knew she hadn't conceived just to bring offense to Christ. When my nap was over, I remembered what God had shown me. That scene felt like it lasted through my entire rest. I began to pray for Mom and that she would give birth to her next assignment.

Mom was enjoying life again, and she no longer needed constant assistance. I now felt comfortable talking to my business partner/sister about our dream to open a salon. We had no idea where to start. We knew that the Department of Business Professional Regulations would provide the licensing we needed, but beyond that, we were at a complete loss as to the next step. We told Mom about our plans, and she was happy for us. She was so enthusiastic about our goals. She found and completed a class on hair braiding. She always braided my hair, keeping it very neat as a child. Before we knew it, Mom was licensed to braid hair professionally. Apparently, she had a plan to be with us in our new shop.

The Lord had been with me those last few years. But, along with the good times and the favor and protection of God had come heartache and disappointments. I didn't know how to accomplish my goals, but I believed God would be the orchestrator just like He'd been in the past. I finished my list of goals and realized it was midnight. I showered and dressed for bed. As soon as I closed my eyes, I saw a white casket, trimmed in pink, and Mom lying there dressed in a beautiful white suit. I recognized the location as the same church that had hosted Dad's celebration of life services.

I quickly opened my eyes and was happy to see that the image was gone. I filed the whole thing in the back of my mind and chalked it all up to being tired and the anxiety associated with my continuous monitoring of Mom's health. Her health was better than it had been in a very long time. I knew she would go home to be with God one day, but not right then. She was a walking testimony to the healing power of God.

A stylist I knew from church operated a salon uptown. I would occasionally go to have my hair professionally styled. Even though I was more than capable of doing my hair, I enjoyed the luxury of relaxing while someone else took care of me. While getting my hair styled that day, my stylist began to say she was moving to another city and she wanted to sell her salon. I couldn't believe what I was hearing! I started inquiring about the price and when she expected to sell the shop. We had to factor in a few things, like would the landlord allow us to sign a lease to continue to rent the building. The wheels in my mind were already turning, but the first thing I needed to do was see what my friend thought.

I called my friend and said, "You're not going to believe what I'm about to tell you! God has just opened a door for us, and my stylist wants to sell her salon!" I could hear screaming on the other end, and she was all in.

We started preparing to purchase the salon and work God's dream in our hearts. The salon officially changed ownership in October 2002. At that time, we began a remodeling project. We wanted to capture the peacefully uplifting vibe we had initially envisioned for our salon. It would take a lot of hard work and money to transform the salon, but we were determined to make it our own. We were ready to invest our time and money into making sure everything was just as the Lord had given us.

The work started, and we were so excited to customize the look of the salon. One of the things I admired about my friend was her creativity. She had an eye for color and a perfect sense of space and theme while remodeling the entire salon. We decided that the waiting area would have chairs and tables, and the multipurpose room would hold a pool table. We thought it would be a good idea for our male customers to be able to pass their time, shooting a game of pool, while they waited for their turn in the barber's chair.

The Lord had given us specific instructions about the atmosphere. He told us not to allow gossip and never to practice negative speaking, but to only have positive and uplifting conversations in the shop. We knew this was going to be an ongoing process. Most people knew where to go to catch up on the latest gossip, and unfortunately, salons and barbershops had always been at the top of that list. But we were determined to create an atmosphere that wasn't offensive yet inviting. We wanted our clients to trust that they would be getting superior cosmetology services in a peaceful environment. They'd just have to catch up on the latest gossip somewhere else.

Mom would frequently pop in during the evenings to cheer on our progress. I couldn't remember the last time I'd seen Mom so excited. I know there were many days when she still missed Dad, but she never complained or refused to quit living.

It was amazing to watch the salon come together. Our families pitched in to help make sure the transition from the old salon to our new peaceful facility went smoothly and quickly.

With the renovations scheduled for completion soon, we decided April 19th, 2003, would be the date of the grand opening of our dream salon. We only had a few months left to plan for the grand opening and tie up loose ends.

While finishing the final touches on the décor, we realized we had not settled on a name for the salon. We began to pray and toss around words and ideas for two weeks. To finalize the state and city licenses paperwork, we had to come up with a name. We couldn't hold a grand opening for an unnamed salon. Love was the center of our theme, and that's all we had. Well, we went to look for supplies at the hardware store for the one-hundredth time, and boom! God dropped the name '*Agape Shears Unisex Styles*' to my sister. The salon's name is strategically aligned with the vision God gave us for the salon. I finished the paperwork, officially becoming *Agape Shears Unisex Styles Corporation*.

We were now down to just a couple of weeks before the grand opening. After doing one last thorough check for items needed, the two barber chairs were the only things left to buy. I invited Mom to go with my sister and me to the supply store. She still liked to be included in everything, and I thought she was due for a lovely Saturday outing. We arrived at the *Salon Depot*, and we were all in awe of their inventory. Everything we could need, they had. We had already looked through one of their catalogs and chosen the barber chairs we wanted. As we approached the cashier to pay for the chairs, Mom turned to me and said, "I'm purchasing one of the chairs for you guys as a grand opening gift." The chairs were expensive, and I didn't want Mom to use her money for such an extravagant purchase. But there comes a time when you can't argue with Mom, and you just say yes, ma'am. We were both stunned by her generosity, and we couldn't thank her enough for her kindness.

Up until this point, God's words had not hit the ground. But somehow, I was struggling to believe that I could do this. I was so nervous about the grand opening, and I was afraid my cutting skills weren't adequate. My business partner had twenty years of experience under her belt, and there I was, a recent barber school graduate. But she was encouraging, and she promised she would help me learn how to become a better barber. While in cosmetology school, the instructors always asked her to assist the other students with their male cuts. She had proven that she was an exceptional barber stylist.

The date and time of our grand opening were finally here. My palms were sweaty, and I kept feeling faint. Whew! There was no turning back now! Our families and friends supported us by supplying the food for our guests. The salon was decorated with balloons, confetti, beautiful lighting, and a new banner with our name printed across it. We wanted everyone to know that something new was happening on the corner. The music was playing, and Mom greeted everyone with a smile when they entered *Agape Shears*.

Our first day of business was a huge success! After the adrenaline was gone, we realized all our strength was gone too! It was a total wipeout, and the only thing that would help us was a good night's rest. God was faithful, and we were barber stylists who owned a salon. Although we were happy, you must know that some people weren't happy for us. Our apparent success threatened them. We had entered a market saturated with seasoned barbers who had been in business in the area for a long time. Our intentions were never to steal their clients. Our thought was that there were plenty of nappy heads needing a cut; there was enough room for everybody.

Part of our dream included working full-time at the salon at some point. Building a loyal, steady clientele would take some time. So, we continued to work our day jobs, and we operated the salon during evening hours and early Saturday morning hours.

We didn't have a receptionist, but we noticed how Mom always showed up promptly at 5:30 every evening with a packed snack. She would settle herself behind the receptionist's desk and greet everybody who came through the door. When the phone rang, Mom would answer it in her most professional voice, set their appointment, and end the call by thanking them and wishing them a pleasant evening. The smile on her face, and the pride she took in keeping the appointment book full, showed us that she loved being a part of the excitement of the salon. She would clock out at 8 p.m., get her things together, and head home. I tried to get her to stay home many days but being there with us was fulfilling. Eventually, I just stopped suggesting that she stay at home and rest. I didn't want to take away the joy and satisfaction she received from helping us build our business. Besides, it gave me a chance to keep an eye on her.

Budgeting was a significant factor while the renovations took place. Of course, we exceeded our budget, and there weren't any funds left for professional advertisement. Word of mouth is always the quickest way to get others to try your goods and services, but we knew being able to add other platforms would be a bonus. We just couldn't afford another platform. Barbering was a profession that men traditionally dominated. We knew some would be skeptical of two female barbers. That didn't stop us from pitching our salon as a great place to experience a fantastic cut in a peaceful atmosphere. Professional advertisements were expensive, but the Lord showed us favor through a local newspaper. A mutual friend of ours was a writer for the newspaper, and she convinced the owner to showcase our grand opening. Once again, the Lord had made a way out of no way for us. He had performed a mighty miracle.

Working two jobs was a first for me. My days started at 9 a.m. and ended at 4 p.m. I would do a wellness check on Mom, then head to the salon. It was a sacrifice, but it was well worth it. I looked forward to 2 p.m. every Saturday. The rest of the day and the following Sunday was a time to relax, go to church, and get ready for the upcoming week.

Mom knew all the right things to say to keep me encouraged. She assured me that we were going to do well. I thanked her for supporting me, even when I didn't understand God's plan. Mother White reminded me that God has a reason for what He orchestrates.

Sundays were for church, even though I could have used a few mornings resting. One Sunday, I cooked breakfast for both of us. Our worship services sometimes lasted over three hours, so it wasn't a good idea to go to church hungry. Eating a good breakfast was the key to holding us over until dinner. After breakfast that Sunday, I went to my house to get dressed. Usually, she'd be dressed and ready to go by the time I got back.

After getting dressed, I went back to check on Mom. As soon as I opened the door to her house, I heard her weakly call my name, "Kamia," she called from somewhere in the house. I could tell something was terribly wrong.

"Where are you, Mom?" I called back to her.

"Over here!" she said. I listened to her faint voice coming from the den area. I ran to the den and found her lying on the floor.

"What happened, Mom? Are you okay?" I asked as I knelt on the floor beside her. I could feel panic rising in my throat. Mom explained that she had spilled water on the floor, and when she tried to mop it up, she slipped and fell. Before I knew it, I had started crying. I felt like it was all my fault. I had left her too soon, and now she had fallen. Her knee was quickly swelling, and its pain registered on her face. I tried to get her up, but I couldn't do it myself without putting too much pressure on her injured knee.

I kept saying that I was so sorry, and it was all my fault. Mom said, "Baby, it wasn't your fault. I should have waited for you to get back over here, then asked you to mop it up for me. Mama was just trying to save you from having to do one more thing for me."

"Mama, I can't do too much for you. I would have mopped that water up and did anything else you needed me to do." Although she was obviously in pain, she didn't want me to call the ambulance. So, I made Mom as comfortable as possible and then called my friend, her adopted daughter, to help me get her up off the floor. She was there in a matter of minutes, and together, we managed to get Mom up. We quickly took her to the ER to assess her injury and get something for the pain.

Before I left the house, I called my dad's sister to let her know that Mom had fallen, and we were on our way to the emergency room. She promised she would forgo her

173

church service and meet us at the hospital. My aunt had been there when my dad was ill, and her loyalty remained the same for Mom.

While driving fast and dodging lights with my hazard lights on, I couldn't help but think that none of this would have happened if I had just stayed a little longer after breakfast.

We arrived at the ER, and my friend ran into the triage desk to ask that someone help us get Mom inside. The hospital sent staff to help get Mom out of the car, into a wheelchair, and into a room. I parked the car and quickly ran from the parking lot back into the hospital. The triage nurse showed me back to Mom's room, waiting on a hospital gurney. Anxiously, we waited for the doctor to come in. I could tell that Mom was in quite some pain, but she didn't complain. My aunt arrived, quietly asked Mom how she was doing, and then did what she could to make sure Mom was as comfortable as she could be in bed. Her presence in the room immediately brought a degree of calm and comfort.

Finally, the doctor knocked on the door then stuck his head into the room. He looked at the triage chart, called Mom by her name, and then asked her what had happened. Mom explained that she'd slipped while cleaning up the water she spilled. Hearing the story again caused me to cry and apologize again to Mom. She grabbed my hand and said, "Baby, it wasn't your fault. Stop crying."

The doctor ordered x-rays to see how extensive the damage to Mom's knee was and determine the best steps to repair that damage. I was thankful for the support of my family and friend. I had spent a great deal of time in the ER with Dad, so those memories occasionally flashed across my mind while sitting in the waiting room.

They gave Mom some pain meds to help manage her pain. I was happy because her knee was really swollen, and I was sure the pain was excruciating. Shortly after that, the x-ray technician came and whisked her away. The whole process took about two hours, then Mom was back, and I knew the doctor would soon follow. A couple of minutes later, the doctor came and confirmed what we thought; she had suffered a broken bone in her knee.

The doctor told us that Mom would need surgery. They needed to place a screw in her knee to repair the break, and I was hoping for a more straightforward way to fix her knee. She had just had surgery a year and a half ago before that, and it had taken so long for her to heal. I think Mom could see the concern on my face, and she quickly responded by reassuring me that everything would be alright. The doctor said the surgery would be scheduled as soon as Mom's Coumadin levels were low enough to clot her blood during the procedure. He estimated that it would take about five days for her levels to reach an acceptable range.

Just when my life had shifted, I experienced another unplanned interruption. I could only pray and hope for the best. The same way God had taken care of me before, I believed He would continue to be faithful and never fail me. Leaving Mom at the hospital bothered me, and I stayed hours after they placed her in her room. I prayed with Mom and left to go home and take care of Crystal, the family dog.

While driving home, I began asking God for strength and protection for Mom. He instructed me to continue seeing Mom every day and let nothing stop me from doing that. He also told me to arrive early enough at the hospital on the day of Mom's surgery to bathe her and pray with her before they would take her to the operating room. My response was, "Yes, Lord. I'll be there every day and arrive early and do what you ask me before her procedure." It had been a long day, and emotionally I was drained.

As soon as I got to work the following day, I spoke with my manager giving details of Mom's fall. I requested that I be taken off the schedule after that Wednesday to be with my mom. He was so considerate and understanding. He knew I was an only child, and Mom needed me for support. I'd called Mom's sister and told her what had happened. I also told her that Mom would need surgery to repair the damage done to her knee. I called out of respect, but I didn't expect her to respond with any urgency. My dad's sister dropped everything to come and help me see about my parents.

I reached out to my out-of-town family and church family to inform them of Mom's condition and the scheduled operation. There I was again, asking for their prayers and support. It hurt to explain what happened to Mom. But I could hear her voice sounding off in the background, telling me that it wasn't my fault. Her words gave me the courage to keep going and do what I did best, love and care for my mom with no guilt.

The orthopedic doctor came to see Mom the Wednesday after her fall. He checked Mom's knee then told us that he had scheduled her surgery for June 6th, at 7 a.m. To ease my mind, he said the procedure would only take an hour, and Mom would be back in her room in no time. For me, anytime anesthesia is involved, it's a critical procedure.

But I appreciated his attempt to ease my concerns about the surgery.

Up until that point, I hadn't seen my mom's sister all week, and neither had Mom. Why hadn't she come to see about her sister? She lived in the same city, and there was no excuse, in my mind, for that behavior! I had always hoped that Mom's sister would heal from her old issues and realize how much her sister cared for her. She had called the Tuesday after Mom's fall, but that wasn't good enough for me. Family should be able to depend on family.

Wednesday evening, Mom's sister stopped by to visit for forty-five minutes. Mom acted as if her sister communicated with her during the hospital stay. Well, not me! Mom was a little more Christ-like than me; I was straight up offended, and I did not attempt to hide it. I walked out of the room and went to one of the public waiting rooms to have a little talk with Jesus. I didn't want Mom to see my frustration, so Jesus helped me get myself together.

The following day Thursday, Mom was in the process of entertaining a room full of visitors. My dad's ever faithful and supportive sister was there, fussing over Mom, and Mom was the life of the party. She was singing, cracking jokes, hugging everybody, and telling her visitors how much she loved them. If Mother White hadn't been in a hospital bed, you wouldn't have known there was anything wrong, let alone that she would be having surgery the following day. Everyone was glad they stopped by to visit with her, and she seemed so happy and pleased to see them.

I stayed with Mom until midnight. By that time, my eyelids were so heavy, and I had that slow blink that children have when they've been up past their bedtime. I knew I needed to be back at the hospital by 5 a.m. that same morning, so I started preparing to leave. Before I left Mom, I would kiss her forehead and rub her head every night. I did the same this night, and Mom thanked me for being with her all week.

I went home, showered, and sat in Mom's recliner. Her baby, Crystal, jumped up in my lap, and I rubbed her head, telling her that Mom would be back soon. I set my clock for 4 a.m., trying to give myself enough time to get dressed and meet Mom at the hospital at 5 a.m. as the Lord had instructed me. My body was tired, but I couldn't sleep. I kept tossing and turning, looking at the clock. After not sleeping, I got up, prayed, and dressed to leave for the hospital.

I arrived at the hospital at 4:30 a.m., and to my surprise, Mom was already awake. We began to talk about the rehab she would need to learn to walk again. The orthopedic doctor had already recommended that she return to the same rehab facility she had recovered in after her bypass. While chatting, I bathed Mom and combed her hair, pulling it back in a neat ponytail. I started telling her how much I loved her and that I'd been praying for her. She reached back, grabbed my hand, and told me how proud she was of me and loved me. I smiled at the irony of our situation. Many years before, it had been me sitting with my back to Mom while she brushed my hair back into a neat ponytail. Now, time had turned our tables, and it was my turn to stand behind Mom and take care of her.

The hospital staff came to get Mom for surgery right at 6 a.m., and I accompanied her to the waiting area where they were to administer the anesthesia. There, we laughed and talked about everything that came to our minds. I wasn't

178

sure if we were talking and laughing so much out of nervousness or confidence that everything would be alright. We had such a good time the anesthesiologist said he didn't want to interrupt us. He laughed along with us for a minute or two, then casually explained his job and how the anesthesia would work. After that, he told us that he would be stepping away to prepare the anesthesia for Mom's surgery. We had about another ten minutes left together before he would return to administer the anesthesia.

Mom and I continued to talk, making plans for her recovery. When the anesthesiologist returned, I prayed for Mom. At the same time, he quietly and respectfully injected the thin needle into the vein in Mom's arm, hung a bag of clear liquid above her bed, and pushed a few buttons on the mobile machine standing beside the bed. By the time I finished praying, he had finished setting everything up, and he was smiling as he watched Mom slowly relax and succumb to the effects of the drugs. Before she ultimately went to sleep, I kissed her and told her I would be waiting for her in recovery. I gathered my things and headed for the door. Before I walked out the door, I turned around, smiled at Mom, and waved. She weakly smiled back at me.

I went to the designated waiting room for families whose loved ones were in surgery. The doctor would come out after surgery, or they would call the room attendant and ask to speak to you if they needed to give you an update. An hour went by, and I was still waiting to hear from the surgeon. Two other families were there, and the surgeons who had operated on their loved ones had already come out and updated them. I was trying to be patient but hoped I would hear something soon.

Just as I stood up to walk to the waiting room door, the phone rang. The attendant called for the family of Helen White. I answered, "I'm Mrs. White's daughter." She gave me the phone, and I heard the surgeon say the surgery was complete. Mom was doing well, and they would bring her to her room in ten minutes, and I could meet them there. I thanked God, thanked the surgeon, and told him I would be waiting in her room.

Once I made it back to Mom's room, I made a few phone calls to my family and friends, sharing the update on Mom with them. I sat in one of the chairs, eagerly waiting for the hospital staff to roll Mom back to her room. While I was waiting, the phone rang, and I answered, thinking they would tell me they were going to the room with my mom. Instead, I heard the worst news of my life. Mom's surgeon said, "I am so sorry to tell you this, but Mrs. White's heart stopped in recovery, and we couldn't revive her."

I screamed, "Noooooooo, This can't be true. Could you try again?!"

He repeated and said, "We tried, but we were unsuccessful."

Shaking, fearful, and at that point, crying uncontrollably, I managed to ask him, "Are you telling me she's dead?" He just continued to apologize over and over. I heard him say that someone would be down to speak with me shortly. I dropped the phone fell to the floor, screaming for God to help me. There was no one there when I received the call that told me my mother was gone. I continued screaming and crying in disbelief that my Mom was no longer with me. All I can remember is how intercession took over for me.

When I came to myself, a nurse was sitting on the floor, holding me and praying with me. She was a spirit-filled Christian, and she told me my prayer language was interceding for my aching soul. It felt like I was in the middle of a terrible nightmare, waiting for someone to wake me. I was numb and utterly void of any understanding of how my mom could have died after they had just told me she was doing great. The pain I felt was paralyzing, and I couldn't move. I sat on the floor in a daze for at least fifteen minutes. When I finally could, I got up off the floor, thanked the nurse who was there with me and moved to sit on the side of the hospital bed where they were bringing Mom back. Before contacting anyone, I sat there in a daze for at least fifteen more minutes.

My dad's sister and my sister-friend were the first to arrive at the hospital. They were crying and hugging me, telling me how sorry they were. I couldn't explain or describe the pain I felt, but their presence meant so much to me I needed someone to lean on and hold me. I convinced myself that God had not left me. It had been less than an hour since I'd gotten that horrible call that let me know my mom was dead, and I was already feeling completely alone.

My aunt and sister began to notify more family and friends of Mom's passing. Shortly afterward, the hospital room was full of people who had come because they were concerned about me.

The surgeon also came by to offer his condolences and apologies. I responded, "Thank you, but I need to see her, Please." He told me that he understood, and yes, arrangements were made to see my mom. He warned me there would still be a lot of blood on her body due to their attempts to resuscitate her. He explained that he would have her body brought to the floor, and the hospital staff would come and lead me to where I could see her.

As promised, a few minutes later, they came and showed me where Mom was. My aunt, friend, and I followed the staff to where they held mom's body. I stood in front of the door, but I couldn't find the strength to open it. My friend reached out and slowly opened the door. *I NEARLY FAINTED* when I came around the corner of the doorframe and saw Mom, 'Mother White.' The little strength I had mustered to stand and walk there left me entirely. Blood was all over her face and hospital gown, and they hadn't removed her breathing tube. I sobbed and screamed as I leaned over her body. I grabbed her hand and said, "I love you, Mama, and I'm so sorry!" I wiped the blood off her cheek, kissed her, and rubbed her head. I just stared at her while I held her hand. For the first time I could ever remember, she didn't grip my hand. I wanted to stay with her, but I knew that wasn't possible. I just needed to see that she was no longer there in the room with me, but she was with the Lord.

"Yes, we are fully confident, and we would rather be away from these earthly bodies, for then we will be at home with the Lord" 2 Corinthians 5:8 (NLT).

Chapter 9

Chapter 9
The Birthing

It had been two days since Mom left this world, and I was a total wreck. I walked around in a fog, oblivious to the passing of time and just plain numb all over. I couldn't gather my thoughts. The task of making funeral arrangements for Mom was overwhelming, and the idea of having to carry on with life without her was unfathomable. Mom had been my compass, and I was drifting, lost without her guidance. If not for Mom's intercession and valuable insight into how she dealt with me, I would have given up and committed suicide long ago. In my heart, I wanted to give her the honorable celebration of life service she deserved. It was vital for me to send her off with dignity and love. I needed to get myself together, one foot in front of the other. You can never thoroughly plan for death.

My family and friends rallied around me, just as they did when Dad died. My cousin/brother came that Tuesday and helped me with the funeral arrangements. Of course, my choir family agreed to provide the music at Mom's funeral, and there was only one choice of who would deliver the eulogy. Mom's beloved pastor, who she had worked with in ministry for twenty years, gladly agreed to honor my request that he preaches at Mom's celebration of life service. As I worked to finalize the arrangements and the outline of the program, people graciously stepped forward and offered their services. I followed the same program order Mom, and I used for Dad's funeral.

During the wake service, I would allow the same time to honor the requests of those who wanted to share how Mom had impacted their lives.

Mom was a retired educator, family leader, and church leader. She was well known for her love for people and the assistance she had given others as they worked to restore their lives and their connection to God. She and Dad often allowed people to live with us as they started their lives. I have never forgotten how freely they opened their hearts and space in our home to people who had nowhere else to go. Many of those people hadn't forgotten either, and they wanted to share the story of the part Mom played in their restoration, spiritually and physically.

Mom and I learned a lot when Dad passed, and I followed the same paths we had taken when it was time to take care of Mom's business. Each morning I tried to come to terms with the fact that Mom was no longer there. I cried everywhere I went as I prepared to bury my last parent, and I was now an adult orphan.

I was given more time off from my job, understanding that I needed to adjust to this unexpected tragedy. The last time I'd spoken to management, the expectations were that I would be taking time away from work to care for my mother, who would be recovering from routine knee surgery. Nothing was normal about what had happened, and my life changed forever.

The whole situation was tragic for me, but it was the greatest gift for Mom. I found comfort in knowing she was now completely healed, with no burdens, no aches, or pains. She was finally living the life she had prepared for while here on earth. She left me with evidence that her God was the only true and living God, and he was faithful, loving, and forgiving. Although my heart was broken and shattered, I knew God was my only hope. There was no way I could make this journey without Him. I hadn't completed the work assigned to my hands, and I didn't know all the plans He had for my life. But I did know I had to find the strength and the peace I'd need to continue the ministry call upon my life.

I didn't sleep much in the days before Mom's funeral. It felt like I was taking cat naps, getting just enough rest to keep pushing forward. I ate just enough to keep from becoming physically weak. Nothing had a taste, but I swallowed a few bites to keep my friends and family from worrying about me. They were closely watching me and always encouraging me to take care of myself while taking care of the heart-wrenching business ahead.

Finally, the weekend arrived, and it was time for Mom's wake. As a gift for Mother's Day, I had bought a beautiful white hat for Mom to wear with her communion outfit. When I purchased the hat, I had no idea that Mom would spend the next scheduled communion day in heaven. So, I requested that the florist make a prop to place Mom's hat on top of the family spray. The finished product was simply stunning, and my breath was taken away by its beauty as I walked to the casket to view Mom's body. The arrangement's beauty was enough to temporarily distract me from that day's purpose. I smiled at how pretty Mom would have thought the whole thing was. But it didn't take long before my attention was drawn from the beauty of the spray, back to the casket which held my mother.

Nothing could have prepared me for that moment. My whole body shook, and I could hear and feel an involuntary wail of sorrow rushing from my belly up through my lips.

Mom was beautiful, and through my tears, I felt God's presence there to support and comfort me. At that very moment, I understood, valued, and appreciated His presence more than I ever had.

I continued to wonder if Mom had left me because she thought I was too busy to take care of her again. I searched my memory, looking for anything I could have possibly said or done that would cause her to think I had something to do that was more important than caring for her. Standing there beside her casket, tears streaming down my face, looking down at her peaceful face, I found nothing, and God's presence eased those thoughts. My brother and sister must have sensed the weight of my emotions lifting from me. They gently guided me to my seat.

A crowd of family members, friends, and former students filled the wake service. It brought great joy to see the compassion and hear many of the stories shared. Mom had touched and influenced more lives than I ever expected. I knew what she meant to me but hearing how much she contributed to the lives of others was comforting. With tears of gratitude for the life of 'Mother White,' some of them stopped to hug me and offer their condolence. She was a treasure to so many.

Saturday finally arrived, and it was time to say my final goodbyes to Mom. Because the facility could accommodate a large crowd, we funeralized Mom at my aunt's church, and they had graciously hosted my Father's Funeral. When we arrived at the church, I couldn't believe the number of vehicles that filled the parking lot, and there were vehicles parked alongside the road and around to the next street. The morning had been stressful, and I was doing my best to maintain my emotional stability.

I had decided not to open the casket at the funeral, but I allowed others to view Mom's body before I entered the sanctuary. I knew the task of trying to start the closure process would be even more challenging if I continued to deal with her death from a physical standpoint. After everyone had left the wake service the previous night, I stayed and sat with Mom. It was at that point that I began my closure. I knew that would have pleased her, and she would have gotten no pleasure from my prolonged suffering and grief.

My family and I entered the church to one of Mom's favorite songs. Everybody was standing, clapping, and praising God to "Can't Nobody Do Me Like Jesus!" The presence of the Holy Spirit filled the room as we came to celebrate the life of a good soldier. I could feel strength added to my soul as I praised with tears falling to the floor. I asked God to help me say something about Mom to touch the listeners' hearts. I was the only one scheduled to speak outside the moderator, eulogist, and those designated to read scriptures.

When the moderator called my name for a split second, I froze. Then I felt the power of the Holy Spirit, and immediately I was able to walk toward the pulpit. The audience was quiet, and I'm sure many of them were concerned that I might not be able to get through my dedication without some assistance. Everyone who knew me personally understood our bond as mother and daughter. Speaking at my Dad's funeral was tough, but I couldn't rate the level of this task on a scale of one to ten if I tried.

I greeted people and acknowledged the clergy and everyone who came to help me celebrate 'Mother Helen Maxine White's life.' There were so many fond memories and teaching moments to choose from, but time would only permit me to share one. After seeking the Lord, He instructed me to share the story of how Mom dealt with the scars on her arms from the bypass surgery. I understood that some people in the audience may not have known the backstory. I explained that Mom needed a bypass, but the veins in her legs weren't medically sound enough to replace the veins in her heart. The doctors used her veins in her arms instead, and the wounds left visible scars. Mom wore long sleeves because her scars drew a lot of unwanted attention. I told how we were getting ready to take a short trip when I noticed Mom was wearing a beautiful short sleeve blouse. I asked her if she remembered she was wearing short sleeves. Her answer was one I'll never forget. She said Jesus had come and visited her. He showed her the scars in His hands and sides from being nailed to the cross. Mom said Jesus told her she didn't need to be ashamed of her scars. They only represented victory, just like His scars represent victory over sin and death. I encouraged people not to allow their blemishes to hold them hostage and not move forward. Jesus died on the cross and shed His blood to forgive them of their sins, and every scar represents victory.

Oh my! The crowd went wild, screaming, crying, and praising God! By that time, I was overwhelmed by the wind of God's spirit, and I began to dance before the Lord. I don't remember how long we were shouting, giving God the Glory. When I came to myself, I wailed because I felt an impartation of my mom's spirit come upon me. There was a shifting in the spirit realm for me after she left this earth. God strengthened me to continue and go further in ministry. Little did I know what God had planned for my life. It was certainly nothing I had expected.

13. "Then he picked up Elijah's cloak that had fallen from him and went back and stood on the bank of the Jordan. 14. He struck the water with Elijah's cloak and said, 'Where is the Lord, the God of Elijah?' Then he struck the water again, and it divided, and he walked over to the other side. 15. The fifty prophets from Jericho saw him and said, 'The power of Elijah is on Elisha!' They went to meet him, bowed down before him" 2 Kings 2:13-15 (TLB).

Our pastor preached an incredible word that honored the Lord and Mom. They approached ministry with the same mindset, and their love for the church, the community, and the choirs blessed many people. Mom also served as the Ladies Ministry President at church, and she gave others a chance to expand their gift of teaching and preaching. In a sense, it was an easy task for Pastor because he knew her well and understood her love for God and people. I was happy and satisfied that we had honored my mother's life to the fullest.

When the service ended, family and friends bombarded me. They wanted to let me know that the story I shared about Mom's experience touched them and reassured them that God had not given up on them. They could recover from faults, bad decisions, or failure by accepting Christ as their savior. During the lowest moment in my life, I was happy to hear the testimonies of those who were encouraged to keep pressing and not give up on God.

8 " If we say that we have no sin, we are only fooling ourselves and refusing to accept the truth. 9. But if we confess our sins to him, he can be depended on to forgive us and to cleanse us from every wrong. And it is perfectly proper for God to do this for us because Christ died to wash away our sins" 1 John 1:8-9 (TLB).

The ride to the cemetery seemed too short. I cried all the way there, asking God to help me with this final step. I now understood when Mom said, "I don't want to leave your Dad in the cold ground." The funeral staff and the pallbearers brought Mom's casket and sat it on the lowering mechanism. My insides cringed, and I wanted to see her face just to touch and kiss her one more time. I fought back the urge to ask if I could see her again. My heart could not have taken the pain of opening and closing the casket. Sometimes in life, we want what's not suitable for us.

I thank God for my brother and sister. They knew I was quickly falling apart under the weight of this final moment. As we prepared to go back to the vehicles, I managed to get close enough to lay my head on the casket, trying to get some relief from the pain I was feeling. They never tried to pry me away or suggest that it was time to leave. They patiently showed the right amount of support and care. Finally, I was able to take that long walk back to the car. The funeral staff drove us back to the church for the repast. Many thoughts were going through my head, and I felt like I would need extra time to deal with losing Mom. The emotional impact of her death was more significant than I could ever put into words.

It had been two weeks since Mom left me. My sister was kind enough to take me to all the appointments needed to close out Mom's business affairs. I was healing, but it probably didn't seem that way to those around me. I was still prone to dissolving in tears at a moment's notice. Everything seemed to remind me of Mom and our time together. I appreciated my sister's patience and the compassion she showed me during that time. The feelings of loneliness often overwhelmed me, and I was so glad to have her by my side.

A few days after Mom's funeral, I received a phone call from a business I had visited and signed paperwork to close Mom's account. Over the phone, the gentleman stated he couldn't close her business because I had failed to sign all the necessary documents. I asked him how that was possible when I had signed every document he presented, and he verified my signature on each of those documents. He refused to take responsibility for the situation or even acknowledge his part in it for some unknown reason. He continued to blame me for the mistakes he made and insisted that I needed to return to his office to complete the process so that he could move forward with closing my mother's account.

I hung up the phone, and all the progress I thought I was making toward healing went straight out the window. Something in the man's voice went straight through my heart. The lack of compassion, the refusal to take responsibility for his mistakes, and the harshness with which he spoke to me were more than I could handle at that moment. Tears began to stream down my face. The path was well-worn and familiar to the enemy, and he saw that I was in a shallow place. I lay in my bed, crying uncontrollably. Then, I heard the door unlock and shut. Three familiar spirits, depression, lack, and fear, walked into my bedroom and began to try and counsel me. They started by declaring that I would not survive my Mom's transition. I had no strength to fight, but my tongues of intercession began to take over. Before I knew it, I was rebuking them and casting them out. I called my sister to explain what had just happened to me. She immediately left her job, and fifteen minutes later, she was sitting by my side. Her face showed the concern she had for my mental health. She did the only thing she knew to do for me; she prayed.

Weeks and months went by, and gradually I felt better and strengthened. God's help, family, and friends played a huge part in my quest to continue living. I wasn't battling against the idea of committing suicide, but I just missed my parents so much that life here on earth felt incredibly empty. There were many days when the pain seemed so overwhelming that tears flowed continuously, tracing that familiar route down my cheeks. I was now living in a season I'd never had to travel, and to try to navigate required supernatural strength. For thirty-seven years, I had a parent here on earth. The comfort that came with having at least one of my parents with me was matchless. After Dad's death, I never gave a single thought to the idea that I would have to live without both parents one day. Because I didn't have any siblings, I highly valued my relationship with my parents. They loved me unconditionally, even during the most challenging and unprecedented moments of my life. When others gave up on me, they somehow believed that I would eventually surrender my life to the Lord again. I watched them love others and give resources to help them start their lives over. No one's parents are perfect, but my parents were perfect for me. The ups and downs I saw them experience helped me know that every trial has an expiration date. It's just a matter of holding on until it expires.

My sister and I continued our dream of providing barber services at our salon. Just thinking of how excited Mom had been about our business venture kept me going most days. Without a doubt, I know she prayed for our continued success. She had spent enough time with us in the salon to make it a place of solace and refuge for me. I felt at peace and incredibly close to her there. So, I looked forward to leaving work and heading to the salon.

I don't know if it's even possible to prepare yourself for the rollercoaster of emotions that comes with returning to church without your parent. Mom and I had worshipped together since I was a child, and her influence and love for God profoundly impacted my life.

I was just fine as I got dressed and drove to worship for the first time without Mom. Several parishioners greeted me with a hug as I made my way to my usual seat as I walked in. I brought plenty of tissues with me in case the tears started to flow. I didn't know what to expect, but I figured I'd probably cry a little bit here and there. From a recent prior experience, I had learned that there was no way to tell when the memories would rush in on me like a flood and break lose the dam of tears I was holding back.

The worship team began to sing, and I lifted my hands to worship. Feeling God's presence was the comfort I needed while walking in this new season. Everything was great until I looked over and saw the empty seat beside me. The realization of Mother White's absence went to another level. Quickly, my truth that God would be by my side was more needed than ever. I sat down and sobbed out of my soul! I could feel the hands and prayers of some of the congregants. The pain felt fresh again, and it was as if I hadn't gained any ground. The dam had broken, and my emotions were out of control, so I decided it would be best to go home before the service ended. Everything had been much harder than I thought it would be. I didn't return to church for another month.

Months passed, and I saw how God was carrying me and helping me maneuver through that season. I was now able to attend church without falling apart. That was a load off my chest, and I knew I couldn't leave my post at church. I felt a personal responsibility to continue in the ministries God called me to impact. I was sure that others missed Mom's singing, clapping, and facilitating Women's Sunday. They often mentioned her contributions to the ministry.

Mom's sister struggled to deal with her death. I knew she was dealing with tremendous guilt and regretting all the lost opportunities to make things right between her and Mom. I also needed healing because I had seen interactions between them that just weren't good, and I still held them against my aunt. Mom always handled them as if she wasn't affected by them. Well, Mom was a little bit more saved than I was! Even though I knew unforgiveness eats away at you, I still had trouble getting past how she had treated my mom. But God had a plan to make sure forgiveness of my aunt made its way to my heart. Eventually, we talked, and I shared my feelings. Still, I would not be handling any pettiness the way Mom had, and I think she knew that.

Before I knew it, a year had come and gone, and life was moving on. My relationship with the Lord was getting stronger. More than anything, I wanted to please Him and offer my life as a living sacrifice. Was I disappointed that my number one cheerleader was no longer there? Of course, I was! But Jesus visited me through a night vision to re-establish His commitment to me.

In my night vision, I walked into the hospital room, and Mom was sitting on the side of the bed, looking beautiful with her shades on. I was so happy to see her, and she asked how things were going for me. My response was, "They're not going well without you!"

Immediately Mom said, "You're going to be just fine." She explained how after the anesthesiologist administered the medication before her surgery, Jesus appeared to her. "Angels came and took me to heaven, and He appeared, asking me if I wanted to stay. I answered no, I must go back and take care of my child and my church family". Mom told me that Jesus responded by telling her that He would take care of us. Breathlessly, Mom explained that everything was so beautiful there, more beautiful than she had ever imagined. Finding it hard to believe, Mom asked Jesus again for assurance that His love and protection would cover her child and the church. Jesus answered her with a 'yes,' and with that, she decided to stay with Him. "I left because I had a promise, and he would take care of you," said Mom.

I woke up from the vision, and the Holy Ghost was all over me. I was crying, speaking in tongues, and worshipping. There was still one question that loomed in the back of my mind. I had always wondered if mom had chosen to leave because she thought I was too busy to take care of her. The vision gave me more peace, and it settled any questions I had about how Mom felt as I cared for her.

My Father in the Lord, my pastor, asked if I would take over as the Women's Sunday Facilitator. Mom had temporarily stayed home with Dad in the past, and I had filled in for her. She trained me to continue while she couldn't participate. But this was huge because Mom wasn't coming back, and I couldn't come home and flood her with questions about what to do next. I would be on my own. My initial response to that opportunity was the promise that I would do my best. I began to pray and ask for supernatural strength to do the job and do it well. Mom knew how to usher in the Holy Ghost, commanding the people to praise God with her. I followed the pattern she left, and God was faithful to me by blessing the people. The church was healing, and, like me, they had finally come to terms with the fact that Mother White was now a soldier gone home to get her much deserved reward.

The clientele at the salon was growing, and my sister and I were working long hours. It was great because being in high demand in the salon meant that I wasn't spending much time at home. My schedule included intercession for others of what God showed me in visions. Honestly, praying was my first love, and I was okay with operating only in that gift. But I knew I had to obey God in all things. Although I wasn't talking about the word given to me by my Father in the Lord about becoming a pastor a couple of years ago, it was still somewhere in my thoughts. It didn't matter. I knew God had not forgotten, but just maybe he would allow me to keep helping at my present church. After all, I had encountered over the last few years; it would seem as though pastoring would and should be the last thing on my to-do list.

I had settled in my mind that I was on the right path at this stage of my life. Attending church was never the same without Mom, but I tried my best to be there serving and worshipping as if things had always been that way. My relationship with God grew stronger and deeper, and I longed to show Him how much I appreciated Him for holding me together.

One morning, I arrived at work as usual, and God began to speak to me. He instructed me to resign from the job I had held for seventeen years. I was stunned and confused. Maybe I was going through something, and deep down, I just wanted to leave my job. I'm far from perfect, but I know when I hear God's voice. I already knew that ignoring Him and pretending I didn't comprehend what He said to me wouldn't change whatever He required of me. But I continued to come to work, and every day I would listen to God say my season there was up. The first two weeks, I simply ignored what I heard and continued to do life. I told myself that it could be His plan for me to leave in the next six months, but He's just preparing me now.

I hadn't discussed what the Lord had said to me with anyone. The truth is, I just didn't want to believe it, so I definitely didn't want to talk about it. Speaking about it would give it credence and validity. Well, God had something in store for me. While counting my drawer one morning, I began to feel His presence. Now that was unusual, and I was caught off guard. God's presence always commands praise. So quietly, I worshipped Him and opened my register, and moved on as nothing had happened. No one had seen me. No one heard me. So, nothing happened!

The following week, the same thing happened again. This time, the strength of God's presence intensified significantly. My hands began to shake, and tears were rolling down my cheeks. Things were getting out of control, and it was getting a little more challenging to hide the effects God's presence had on me. Still, I quickly recovered and put the whole incident behind me.

I felt like I had episodes of God's fire that third week. I was crying uncontrollably and frequently. I could no longer quickly and secretly recover from the encounters. I had to actually leave the floor and step into the restroom to gather myself. The message hadn't changed: "Your time has come to an end here." My co-workers and the customers were concerned because I was a wreck, but I continued working. God's fire was like a faucet pouring hot coals over my head.

After work, I called my sister to explain what I had been experiencing. She was shocked and concerned. After I had described everything that had happened to me, she simply asked about my resignation letter. That certainly wasn't what I expected her to say. I wanted her to try to convince me that I was just exhausted from working my regular job and then working late into the night at the salon. She could have acted as if God didn't want me to quit yet. But she didn't spare me, and she didn't encourage me to run from what was clearly inevitable.

I finally started talking to God about the matter, and I asked if I could just have a little more time. I didn't get an immediate response. A few days later, the morning had begun pretty well. I dressed for work, grabbed some breakfast, and headed to the job. Once there, I greeted my colleagues and went to my station. So far, so good! Oh, but a couple of hours later, I started having severe pains in my chest, and my breathing was affected. I felt like 'Fred Sandford'; maybe the uneasiness I experienced were signs of a heart attack. My supervisor wanted to call the ambulance to get me and transport me to the hospital, but I declined and called my sister to take me to the ER.

When I arrived at the hospital and described my symptoms to the triage nurse, they immediately rushed me back for a series of tests. I had explained all the usual signs of a heart problem. My blood pressure was higher than expected, and that scared me. They ran several tests, and everything was negative. The doctor ruled out a possible heart attack or stroke based on the results of the tests. After observing for two hours, my blood pressure registered 120 over 72. The doctor told me to go home, take a few days off from work, and follow up with my primary physician. I thanked the doctor and told him I would do as he ordered.

After the doctor signed off on my chart and left the room, the nurse began to get my orders together and unhook me from the monitoring machines. While she was working, she turned around and looked me straight in my eyes and said, "Ms. White, what's weighing on your mind?" I sat up on the side of the bed, and my head hung low. I couldn't even look at her. "Whatever it is, just let it go, and you'll be fine." OMG! Now God is telling the nurse to diagnose my problem and solve it! She took a step closer to me, and when I lifted my head and looked at her, she simply said, "Let it go!"

I couldn't avoid her eyes or ignore her without seeming incredibly rude. "You are right. I had a panic attack because I'm not following the Lord's instructions." She didn't say another word, and she just nodded and left the room.

I arrived home, dazed and a little tired. I couldn't believe this was happening to me! Knowing that God would not be satisfied until I submitted to His will. I sat down and began to plan how I would resign.

I got up and fixed some coffee with a light breakfast the following day. I turned on the television to watch my favorite Christian station. Listen! The Lord even controlled the message I saw and heard that day. As soon as I turned on to that station, the preacher said, "Hey you! God said your season is up! Speak to your management and give them your resignation. I know you don't understand but obey God and prepare for transition!" I was startled and couldn't move. The pastor who was preaching on the TV was pointing straight ahead, and it was as if he spoke directly to me. Now God has highjacked my program! I couldn't seem to get away from His words.

I plopped down in my chair and began to say, "Yes, Lord! I can't run from your presence." I don't understand when people say God won't make you do His will. I beg to differ! He knows how to get a yes if that's what He wants in that season. He doesn't negotiate with us but squeezes our purpose out of us. I acknowledged all that.

"If you want favor with both God and man, and a reputation for good judgment and common sense, then trust the Lord completely; don't ever trust yourself. In everything you do, put God first, and he will direct you and crown your efforts with success" Proverbs 3:4-6 (TLB).

A week later, I requested a meeting with my supervisor and handed in my resignation letter on a Monday. The pastor on the program said they would try and change my mind because I was a great employee, and they didn't want to lose my skills. He was right, and my supervisor asked me to think about it for a few days. She promised she would work with me with any of my requests. I AGREED TO DO AS SHE SUGGESTED because I loved my boss and had worked with her for the entire seventeen years of my employment there. I would give it more thought. I knew there was no changing my mind; God's instructions were sealed in my heart, and there was no way to deny it.

I worked a few more days without God's overwhelming presence hovering over me, causing a flow of tears and tongue talking. He hadn't left me, but He got what He wanted: obedience. I never asked God why I needed to go away from a place I'd been for seventeen years, and it didn't interfere with my daily routine. I continued to work at the salon, go to church, and figure out what could be next. The whole thing felt weird to me, and I struggled with deciding to leave, but I had no choice.

Hurricane season was among us, and it was impossible to determine the outcome that year. There had not been an intense storm in our area for quite some time. Hurricane season is always from June to November, and a significant storm hit us in June of 2004. Wind damage and flooding left many homes without electricity. Our pastor postponed services indefinitely until things improved. My house was without electricity for a little over a week. They repaired the wiring, but I only received partial power after a day. I had never seen that issue arise in my years of living in the area and having storms.

I started checking on family and friends to see how they were doing after the storm. Everyone was experiencing different scenarios, and some had no power for two and half weeks. Can you imagine living in sweltering heat and not keeping any food in the house due to no energy? Many families were going through severe difficulties, and they had no way of changing their present situations.

One of our church families had become victims of the storms, and they were in dire need of assistance. They had filled their refrigerator with food after the restoration of power. While they were at work the next day, another power outage occurred. By the time they arrived home from work, all the food in the refrigerator was spoiled. They were understandably devastated those bad conditions destroyed two weeks of food supplies. The temperature in their house was so hot they had no choice but to spend several nights in a hotel. It was an expensive but worthwhile decision.

Eventually, the energy company restored power at their home, and they gladly returned to their house. While they no longer had to pay for a hotel, the new problem was that they didn't have money to buy food. One of the family members asked the church for a loan to purchase food, and the church was financially able to offer a loan. Unfortunately, the information given to the church's chief financial trustee wasn't the truth. After hearing the need for the loan, the officer rejected the inquiry.

I was so surprised and disappointed that the church turned down an opportunity to help the family during a crisis. Sitting at home digesting the situation, the Lord impressed my heart to buy as much food as possible for the struggling family.

The decision to deny the family's application for assistance based on false information was disturbing and devastating. I was heartbroken, disappointed, and ashamed of how we, the church, handled the need of this family.

The following Sunday at church was nothing I had ever experienced, and it felt like a spiritual cloud hovering over the church. Years ago, at a church I visited, the leaders refused to allow the Holy Spirit to bless the people; accordingly, this felt the same. I began to weep and travail so violently that I finally had to go outside to avoid being a distraction. The decision of the financial trustees weighed on my soul, and I couldn't relieve myself of the pain I felt. I have always been sensitive to the move of the Holy Spirit, and this day He was grieved.

Before the service concluded, we would have a chance to request prayer. I made my way to the front of the church because those feelings of unrest covered me like a blanket. How could I continue to worship with people who refused to help bring relief to one of their own? I was first in line for prayer, and my Spiritual Father laid his hands upon my head as the tears rolled down my face. He leaned in toward me and said, *"The Lord says for you to do and go wherever He tells you. For I, the Lord God, am with you!"* While he was praying, my Spiritual Father never asked the Lord to heal my heart. While he wasn't part of the decision to deny assistance to that needy family, I'm sure he was aware of the hurt that decision caused. Because of the authority of a spiritual parent, I'd never had to share most of my prayer requests. Spiritual parents can see into the soul of their spiritual children. Although the words he spoke to me seemed different, I never questioned what he meant by those words.

The next few Sundays were hard for me. I couldn't stop crying during the service, and the heaviness I felt just wouldn't go away. I tried everything to act so that I didn't bring attention to myself. It appeared that I was the only one still in a place of uneasiness and disappointment. Finally, I concluded that I had to fall on my face before God and not get up until I received relief.

As soon as I hit the floor, lying prostrate, the presence of God wasted no time showing up. I began to repent for the feelings of being disconnected from my church. I loved my Spiritual Father, and I pledged to the Lord that I would always honor him and help him. He was bold and fearless while exemplifying that he wanted nothing other than to save my soul from hell. When many others had given up on me, he never did. He was always kind and encouraging, constantly reassuring me that God would restore me. I'm confident that my mom and pastor's prayers kept the devil from taking my life while I was a wreck. So, I knew that I just needed emotional healing from the whole situation. I was sure that God would reach into my soul leave the peace of mind, the love, and the help I needed to re-establish the level of commitment I once had.

After bawling my eyes out for almost an hour, my spirit making intercession for me, the Lord finally spoke. He began by letting me know that what I felt had nothing to do with the church. In a very familiar voice to my heart, the Lord spoke to me and said, *"I allowed it to happen to bring you to a place of humility. I was seeking an audience with you. You were opened to serving me but not in total obedience. The disconnect you are feeling is coming from Me. The word was spoken to you by your Spiritual Father that there is Pastoral Call was upon your life. Since that time, you have not acknowledged it, and you have not prepared for the transition. The pain you've come through opened you to hear my voice out of desperation. I orchestrated it all to bring you to a place of obedience."*

I lay there for another hour because I couldn't see how the transition would occur. There was a who, what, and where thought process in my mind. Why would the Lord ask me to do something this weighty without letting my mom stay here to help me? She would have been so instrumental in helping me accomplish this task. The Lord reminded me of a vision I had of Mom being pregnant eight months before she died. I had some of the revelations of that vision, but other parts were still unclear. I now had the complete interpretation of that vision. It included my giving birth to a baby, meaning the church. It also told me that I would face opposition to what God called me to do. Mom's job called her to conceive and start carrying the baby, meaning a new purpose to the eighth month. And I would give birth to it, bringing it into fruition.

Once I understood the call, I answered the Lord with a yes. If He was willing to help me accomplish the call, I was finally ready to go. The truth had always been that I only wanted to be an intercessor and a drummer, and Pastoring was never one of my desires. But I loved God so much, and I didn't want to make the same mistake I made twelve years prior.

A couple of weeks later, I requested a meeting with my Spiritual Father. I was so nervous about it, and I had no idea how to explain my heart to him. God is so incredible, and I am convinced that He prepared my Spiritual Father for my visit. The palms of my hands were sweating, and my mouth felt desert dry. In my heart, this was one of the hardest things I had to do since accepting the deaths of my biological parents.

I arrived at church a little early to pray for the strength to share my heart. When I finally sat in the room with my Spiritual Father, the conversation started with me saying how much I loved him and appreciated how he risked his reputation and relationships to revive me. I realized that he went through a great deal of difficulty because he loved and believed in me. True loyalty is a rare quality, and I wanted him to know I would never forget his kindness.

Pausing for a few seconds after a big sigh, I told him that God called me to start a ministry. While I was saying those words, I could feel the water rising in my eyes. I blinked a few times, and tears began to fall before I could finish the sentence. I couldn't help but feel that I was forfeiting my loyalty to him. The whole time I was speaking, he listened very attentively, making me feel as comfortable as possible. It felt like he was already aware of the purpose of my meeting with him.

Surprisingly, he said he waited for me to talk with him about it when I finished speaking. He reminded me of the Sunday I came up for prayer. That day he revealed to me God's plan for my life. He said he released me to go and follow God's leading. Some years ago, my Spiritual Father said when God was ready for me to carry out His plans of pastoring, He would get my attention.

He was a true Prophet! God had stopped me in my tracks, and I had no choice but to listen to His plans for me. My Spiritual Father explained that my love for him had nothing to do with God's plan. He knew the day would come, and he did not question my loyalty. My Spiritual Father told me that God is with me, and pleasing God was what I needed to do. He promised me that he would be alright, and there was no need to worry while pursuing the Lord's following. It all seemed unreal, but I was willing to follow God with his blessing. That day I gained an even greater respect for my Spiritual Father and his love for his spiritual children, releasing them into their destiny.

Only a mature Spiritual Parent could see the value of raising someone and sending them to fulfill their call without slander. I will never forget how my Spiritual Father handled me in every season of my life.

Chapter 10

Chapter 10
Lucifer's Replacement

Uncharted waters would be the best way to describe starting a church. Being a minister, prophet, teacher, evangelist, or associate pastor is not the same as being a senior pastor. Over the years, seeing the chief executive leader's many challenges always made me happy that I didn't have that responsibility. But you know Jesus also had a hard way to go and did I think anything had changed. You are dealing with so many personalities, and some have many reasons why they are part of a church. Some days I felt like I was in a trance trying to see how to work the plan of God. Deep down, I was scared, and my mind was all over the place trying to get it together!

My Spiritual Father said to inform him when the Lord was ready for me to launch the ministry. He made the executive decision not to announce my ordination. We both knew that there would be strong opposition from many at the church. Since Mom's transition, the cohesiveness was not the same among the members. It was apparent Mom's presence was vital to my Spiritual Father, myself, and a few others. The spirit of Jezebel was running rampant and causing a great deal of confusion. I knew many would feel that I was leaving due to the incident during hurricane season. But it didn't matter what we said, and they labeled me as a rebellious person who split the church.

Leaving my Spiritual Father was never thought of because of my love for him, and I was loyal to him for the ridicule he received while saving my life. Not many Spiritual Parents recognize that God is birthing a leader out of them, and some see God's plan but will not release their mentees into their destiny without slander. It was a tremendous blessing to serve a leader who walked in humility and understood the Apostolic call upon his life, raising others to continue the work of God.

After much prayer and consideration, God gave me a time frame of six months. I arranged a meeting with my leader to discuss the possible timing, and he encouraged me and set the ordination for the following Sunday. Oh Lord, Have Mercy; I wasn't expecting it so soon! We were still in 2004, but he assured me there was no need to wait, for God had spoken.

I decided not to share this move with anyone at church out of respect for my leader. I told two other friends who were not members, and they chose to come for support. My Spiritual Father said the Lord told him others would go with me to help, and he was aware and excited. He said I've taken you all as far as I can. If anyone was going to be part of the vision, I wanted them only to be influenced by the Lord. Everything needed to be done in order as much as possible. Unfortunately, no matter how much my Spiritual Father and I would explain this stream of events, no one was buying that God had called me to lead. I tried to be prepared as much as possible for a fallout. I wanted to protect my leader from the backlash and hate he would receive for releasing me with his blessing with everything in me. He repeatedly said not to worry because God had anointed him for this season in my life. After that, I stopped questioning whether he would be okay; I had to trust God that my Spiritual Father was also in His hands.

The entire week leading up to the ordination made me think of why God would require this of me now. Those thoughts continued since He began the chase, resulting in a yes from me. I admit my confidence was low, and I had no idea how pastoring would turn out for me. But, if He did it for Peter, He could do for me! I loved God so much and didn't want to disobey Him, even if it meant trying to walk on water.

"8 This plan of mine is not what you would work out, neither are my thoughts the same as yours! 9 For just as the heavens are higher than the earth, so are my ways higher than yours, and my thoughts than yours Isaiah 55:8-9 (TLB).

I lost five pounds that week due to not having an appetite. My stomach was in knots most of the time. There comes a time in your life that you take chances because you believe the word spoken over your life. As I reflected on many past situations, God was low-key training me, and I hadn't noticed it. There was so much I could have learned, but I resisted opportunities to develop further as a leader. But God was faithful, speaking wisdom and clarity as I prepared for this next shift in my life.

Saturday before Sunday, I went to the church to lay before God. I didn't have many words, just one prayer request. 'Be with me, Lord; I can't do it without you.'

Sunday morning had arrived, and I was so nervous my hands were shaking, and I could barely get dressed. I played the scene of the ordination in my head a thousand times.

Each time the images were full of tension and unbelief. I knew there would be very few that believed I was following God's Will for my life. But my Spiritual Father's affirmation of me was enough for me to move forward. I chose to wear black, not because I was sorrowful, but because black symbolizes power. The call of God required strength and humbling yourself before Him. As the time came closer for my Spiritual Father to announce this special event, I began to pray for strengthened knees and pray for him as well. My entire body seemed as if it was getting weaker by the moment. While tussling back in forth, I rebuked the barrage of feelings and battled, sending a note saying I had changed my mind.

Finally, the moment was here, and he called my name, and I slowly walked to the front and stood beside him. All eyes were on me as the crowd wondered what was about to happen. My Spiritual Father addressed the audience confidently with the Lord's word given to him that day for me as I drove him to an engagement. He confirmed that now was the Lord's timing to accept the call to become a Pastor. He never asked any of the leadership team to address his decision. They were intentionally left out, and there was no chance for them to deny his affirmation. At this point, my back was facing the congregation, and I could hear and feel some people's anguish as my Spiritual Father prayed and laid his hands on me as an outward sign of his blessing and ordination. Darts hurled in the spirit to offset my receiving the approval of my Bishop. But God blocked them, and the manipulators were disgusted that there was no time to overthrow my destiny.

When the service ended, I was approached by those who opposed the ordination. The members bombarded me with questions and looks that could kill me. The opposers accused me of being my Spiritual Father's favorite, and he would agree to anything I said. So, it was apparent they did not believe that it was not my idea to take this position but the Lord's. I knew validating the next chapter in my life would create a war zone for him at home and church. I knew my Spiritual Father was about to face mixed emotions due to the pain, and it kept me on my face before God petitioned for him.

You would have thought Jezebel would be happy that I was gone. But I learned that it causes them to be even more disgruntled if they cannot control you. The spirit worked unbelievably hard to discredit my influence on others by constantly keeping my past sins before them. My mom was the reason they tolerated me. Her passing was significant, so I would begin to walk in the next season even If I did not want to go.

Some asked me the date of the first service. At that time, I did not have an answer. I knew some would transition because I saw it in a vision. I waited for God to reveal His plans to those who He sent to help. I could not wait to get in my vehicle and take a deep breath. Tears streamed down my face as God reminded me of the vision of Mom's pregnancy. She started a ministry, but I would give birth to a church on a larger scale. Mom said, "He would be with me."

As I continued to push past my fears of this role, I began to feel that teaching the truths about sexual perversion was part of God's plan. However, based upon the uproar of a preacher, backslidden, and now saying God called them to Pastoral leadership was a great deal to swallow for most.

After the ordination service, I remained a member and decided to do so until God gave me a date and a name for the church. Some Sundays, I would visit, leaving knowing that the sermon preached was for me. I was struggling with my confidence, but I knew I heard the voice of God to move forward with His plans for my life. I began to seek God for more instructions. One day I drove to get some lunch, and while in the drive-thru, I heard the Lord say name the Church *' Reviving Souls Ministries'*. I asked God why it didn't sound like a name for a church. His response was, ***"the name represents who I have called you to be in this season, and you will revive souls back to me."*** The light bulb popped on after that. I fully understood the call to help those who had walked away from God just like me and needed help navigating back to God.

The doors of Reviving Souls opened on March 6, 2005. Those God had spoken to help me in ministry began to confirm their commitment. My friend of twenty years at that time also came with a guest to support me. God had provided everything I needed to fulfill His plan for ministry. The Lord was very faithful, and His Presence validated that I obeyed His will for my life. Many testified after the service ended how encouraged they were and the blessings they received.

After a few weeks went by, the Lord showed me a minister from my Father in the Lord's congregation who tried to slander me and sabotage Reviving Souls. In a night vision, the Lord revealed the minister speaking with another Pastor, trying to cause strife by spreading lies about me and defying Bishop's Authority to ordain me. It just so happens I was given a word of knowledge for the same Pastor in the night vision. I called the Pastor to encourage them, but the Lord didn't allow me to mention the minister scandalizing me. After hearing the word of the Lord, the Pastor revealed the minister who tried to scandalize my name. Once again, grace covered me. If we are doing what God has called us to do, we won't have time to try and tear someone else down. I believe it is essential always to remain humble, staying in God's Presence. Although you may have moved on in your life, others are still angry with you and will do anything to disrupt God's plan.

After being in that location for almost two years, we received a letter that stated we must have permission from the city to open a church. I consulted with other local Pastors, and they had never heard of such an ordinance. So I began to ask what was required to receive approval from the city. God had gone before me and provided a man who measured our parking lot and paid for the architectural plans needed. He also knew someone on the board, so I had to show up to the meeting answering a few questions, and it was approved. God blocked the enemy's plans again! Halleluiah!!!

Many in the Christian community loved our praise and worship. But some did not want to hear about God's love and deliverance power as it related to the LGBTQ community. The plight of homosexuality in the church was not something people wanted to listen to; it was still taboo. I believed my story could help others who had heard people's opinions on the matter, but not absolute truths. Finally, I came to terms that my call was unique. I concluded that my position was not just about those who followed Christ but those in bondage trying to follow Christ.

Reviving Souls supported offering help to reach gay, bisexual, and transgender people. I had a special place in my heart to share love, truths, and not hate. I remembered all too well my experience with some of the Christian community while I was away from God. We did not see the LGBTQ community as a lost cause, as the church sometimes alluded. But we saw it as an opportunity to encourage others and share our own experiences with sexual struggles. You know, it is almost impossible to give others hope without condemnation, figuring into the conversation when you have not experienced one's walk of life. I believe God has anointed some to make a huge difference without the same experience by simply remembering we all don't sin the same, but we all have sinned, needing God's forgiveness and love.

I often shared my testimony when prompted by the Holy Spirit. When God ordained this, a great move of His Presence would sweep through the church and the altar filled with people who were sincere and cried out to God for help. My heart would just swell with joy as I prayed with God's people. I knew their fight and the shame they felt in their heart from participating in lifestyles that did not agree with God's plan for our lives. But the struggle to change and be consistent was more complicated than just coming to the altar. A commitment to evolving conversations, protecting our eye-gates, and limiting relationships where weakness could overtake us was a must until we could resist the urge to go back to our past.

In 2009, the Lord also started a new evangelistic service called 'Sunday on Tuesday!' We had bible study on Wednesday and Sunday services until that time. I was sitting in service when I received the new download from God. He said, "there are many Bible studies available for people to attend, but there are no evangelistic services during the week unless they host a revival. I want my people to know I will save, set free, and heal during the week!" WOW, God! It took

216

me for a loop! I had not realized how people waited for a Sunday service to experience a move of God.

We were excited to start this new phase and offer others healing, strength, salvation, and deliverance. During this time, the Prophetic Psalmist anointing birthed into our atmosphere. I was incredibly proud of our praise and worship leader and how she responded to being trained to sing prophetically. During this season, she learned how to hear God and sing what He wanted to hear. She and I and the other singers worked as a close team to give words of wisdom to attendees. Some thirty years ago, I received this impartation from another prophetic ministry. God told me I would see it again, and I never thought He would use the gift in a church led by me.

We began to advertise our new service as the 'Kavod,' "No More Church as Usual!" *"This new house will be more glorious than the former, declares the Lord of Armies. And in this place I will give ⌐ them ¬ peace, declares the Lord of Armies " Haggai 2:9 (GW).*

We also changed our dress code to jeans, blouses, tees to attract those who did not have dress clothing for church. The first night we saw visitors, friends, and clergy. I will never forget that night! It felt as if we were in a revival or a conference. God revealed to me that when people expect the 'KAVOD' the Glory of God, there will be a heavy encounter of God's Glory. Some laid on the floor, some sobbed uncontrollably, while others danced. Our minds were blown away by how God's Presence overwhelmed the house. Now we began to understand better why the changes to our church format. The 'Kavod' wanted to be the main attraction.

217

Word of mouth spread throughout our community, and people came from all over.

God had no respect of persons at 'Sunday on Tuesday' anyone who wanted in encounter received it. But some became part of Reviving Souls because they were free to talk about the struggles with sex as a single person. We continued to see increased attendance at our 'Sunday On Tuesday.' services. People were coming from outside the county to have an encounter with God. The word began to travel that you could go as you were. Condemnation didn't have a place at the service, but truths preached to set the captive free.

Some received their prayer language and went back to their home churches to be better followers. We saw a glimpse of how people can come together from different churches and denominations in unity and experience God's corporate move. Although we witnessed the joy of the Lord every time we gathered, it was not without a price. Some Pastors were having an issue with their members joining us on Tuesdays. Reviving Souls was now the topic at other bible studies, leaving their members feeling condemned for coming.

At first, I was hurt and could not understand how people would rather see their members stuck rather than healed. Some Pastors sent other members to the service as spies to see what was happening. I never tried to recruit visitors to be part of Reviving Souls; I only pushed them to Jesus. It had been almost twenty years since the Community Choir started and faced the same politics. Unfortunately, it was a reminder that things had not changed.

In 2010, I began to pray about doing a seminar to teach God's truths about homosexuality. Never in a million years would I have thought that God would use my failures to help others succeed as victorious. If I had listened to others, I would have hidden my season of indulging in sin without conviction or the thought of repentance. The Bible clearly states that *"God puts people right through their faith in Jesus Christ. God does this to all who believe in Christ because there is no difference at all: everyone has sinned and is far away from God's saving presence." Romans 3:22-23 (TLB).* So, the notion that God has sin on a scale is frivolous. Why should I be ashamed of the grace and mercy extended to me by God?

The task of organizing and inviting others to the event was constantly on my mind. Although I would see many people struggling with homosexuality in churches I visited, I wasn't sure they would attend a public seminar about it. Because with the church, 'do not ask do not tell policy was in effect.' So, registering for the event could be interpreted as being guilty of the gay lifestyle.

After much prayer and study, I planned the seminar inviting leaders and participants in the arts ministry. Over the years, I began to recognize that those in the arts, such as music ministry, dance ministry, serving ministry, and other creative gifts, seemingly were tempted to lead a lifestyle of homosexuality more than other church gifts. So, I intentionally targeted them.

The one-day event was named 'Too Hot for Church!' Yes, I already know it was wild and not for the spirited religious saints. The title alone made many feel we were a bit too out there to help anyone. But the truth of the matter was many could identify with the title even if they remained silent. Their thoughts about gay life were every day, yet they continued to stay faithful. Deep down, I had experienced the trying to keep going mindset, and somehow this was a phase I was going through. I wanted freedom from the repeats of going back. So, we named it 'Too Hot for Church' to declare that we would expose the enemy's tricks against us.

Six weeks before the seminar was scheduled to occur, I suffered what I believe was a warfare attack against my body. The attack was so severe I was unable to attend church for five weeks. My bronchial area was compromised, and breathing was a chore. My equilibrium lost its proper function, and fever racked my body on and off. Finally, the doctor prescribed antibiotics, breathing treatments, and steroids. I had never been that ill with bronchitis before. Thank God for a praying church because, at one point, I felt like I would not live.

I began to feel much better and ready to move forward with God's vision. Eight people signed up, including two leaders. One leader requested my notes because they were too embarrassed to attend, and my answer was no; you would have to join the session in person. Then, of course, we started the event with worship, and oh my God! The Presence of God overwhelmed us, which confirmed that this was the right thing to do. I was grateful for the confirmation, and it calmed my nerves.

The subject matter was considered by many to be too obscene to discuss in the church. Why? Many of the saints discussed situations and used condescending names behind closed doors. They did this to label those and forgot that they had earned a title as well, more like a 'GOSSIPMONGER!'

I prepared handouts and explained the definition of sexual perversion according to God's boundaries. The love of God surrounded them as they listened attentively. There was

220

no condemnation or shame. Some shared their experiences as they felt more comfortable as we shared ours. We cried, we worshipped, and we shouted, knowing that the truth had impacted our lives and strengthened us to walk closer to our God. We had such a great time; we stayed together long after class. Some gave great testimonies about how the information they received blessed them and gave them more hope to live beyond their prior knowledge. After hearing the class critic, I rested assured that we had done our best to complete the assignment to encourage others. Although the number of registrants did not meet my expectations, I was pleased that God was pleased. Over the years, I have learned that quality can be more crucial than quantity.

Watching others grow and use their gifts was my desire. I often thought about my early years in ministry, and if I had more guidance, I would have handled opposition better. When people inquired about joining Reviving Souls, I met with them and discussed their childhood. This information would help me understand their behaviors linked to trauma or disappointment in their early lives. I was always curious why some people found it more challenging to follow than others.

Abandonment and rejection were our biggest enemies as we began to grow. Individuals who have not received emotional healing in those areas will be limited in their ability to follow and take constructive criticism. When I looked back at the churches I had previously been a member of, it was evident that there were saints in bondage and created chaos for others. The senior leader met head-on with many members whose emotions led them rather than truths.

They often competed against their spiritual brothers and sisters for attention. At times it felt like these were kids in adult bodies. The interviews were vital and usually determined their spiritual growth.

We continued to do ministry the way God led us. I will admit our formats were not conventional. The Presence of God would come in like a whirlwind and completely take over the service. Many nights I didn't stop to read a scripture to preach a sermon. God powerfully used the worship team, making my job easy. Under the tutelage of Mother White, I learned that God was the orchestrator of our services, and I gave up my plan to please God. Many attendees encountered the Presence of God in ways they had not experienced.

We became cheerleaders and praised people while they were walking out their deliverance. It reminded me of support groups and how they encouraged the participants. For example, one night, one of our single mothers said she had gone without sex for ten days! She previously shared that the most she had ever been without sex were two days. Boy, did we tear up the place with our pom-poms, screams, and a good shout! Someone else would have thought this should not be part of a church service sharing sensitive information. But I believe because she revealed her struggle without condemnation, it didn't bother her or us that she shared her progress.

In 2012, Reviving Souls hosted our first two-day conference call 'Ex-Ho Expo,' a success. We decided to change our venue and the county to give others a chance to attend. We planned an agenda that focused on worship and the truths about sexual perversion. The first night included praise teams, dancers, and spoken word! It was an absolute party for Jesus! Many shared they hadn't experienced a conference that tailored worship and education. God exceeded my thoughts of success and Pastors brought their teams to experience the worship and teachings. I was completely overwhelmed by God's Faithfulness.

Seeking God was not a chore but valuable to my life, strength, and how I operated. But unfortunately, the enemy never sleeps or takes a break when it comes to creating chaos. After an enormous breakthrough, the ministry attacked, and some spiritual casualties occurred. I was devastated, and clearly, the enemy devised a plan.

Reviving Souls would experience another incredible blessing in 2012. A couple visited one of our Sunday on Tuesday services. One of our Pastors invited them, and they also pastored a local church nearby. I believe that the Lord penetrated their heart during the service and gave them a great love for what we were doing. The Holy Spirit filled the room as we worshipped that night.

A couple of days later, I went to lunch with the Pastors. He began to offer their multipurpose room on their campus as another place to host more people for our events. I was stunned that these two beautiful Caucasian Pastors wanted to help me. Weeks later, while planning for our fellowship's General Assembly, our hotel was unavailable the first night. I approached the Pastors to rent their facility, and they were thrilled to oblige my request.

We were excited to have churches from all over be with us that weekend. While setting up Friday morning, I saw one of the Pastors, and they were bubbly with excitement. God had spoken to them, and this place would be our home for the church if we wanted. I almost passed out and asked: "are you serious?" What an absolute miracle! It was everything I wanted to help us expand our ministry. The interesting thing is two weeks before meeting the Pastors; I asked a builder for an estimate to build a stage. What a mighty God we serve! He gave me my heart's desires.

November 11, 2012, the Pastor brought over their box truck and moved us to their facility with a stage and kitchen. The move began a shift in my life that I had no idea was coming. I've always desired to follow God's direction in ministry and personal life. There has been plenty of unrest and not fully understanding His lead, but I pressed to do it His way. Sometimes, understanding the will of God and having faith doesn't always match. On many occasions, I felt like Abraham when God said, leave what you're accustomed to and venture to the new place I have prepared for you. Going isn't always physical, but it's a mindset that you must be willing to leave behind.

God moved us from our initial physical start in the ministry; He also changed the audience who attended our services. I can't explain how that happened, but those who once participated stopped. At first, I didn't understand it, but God changed my audience, and the move was part of a unique plan to reach other cultures. We also had begun to sing at a local outdoor festival that placed us in a different environment, but it was one of the best things that could have happened. The Lord was broadening our scope of ministry. So that we follow God's plan, some doors must be closed.

Some parishioners were not happy about the Pastor's decision to allow us to worship on their campus. The Lord validated the move through a night vision amid uncertainty. He visited me, and I saw three three-foot tall spiders with orange stripes on their legs attacking me. Spiders in a dream mean that the timing of the next phase or assignment is under sabotage by the enemy. As the spiders tried to strike me, Pastors in Reviving Souls fought them. One of the Pastors had a white-colored can of spray, and they began to spray a white midst all over the spiders, and they died. God prevailed, and the angry parishioners could not overturn the Pastor's decision decided by their States Conference Bishop.

The campus Pastor came up with a fantastic idea to do a fellowship with all the churches on the campus. What a God idea, and it proved to be a game-changer. We participated in the worship singing, and the Lord touched many of the hearts in the congregation. I helped serve communion, and the service began tearing down the wall of resistance to our presence on the campus. The Presence of the Lord flowed as we sang, and some even cried.

While on this new journey, the Lord began to give me a huge burden for women. It was all clear now that my early temptation to live as a lesbian was more apparent than ever. Why would women want to hear a woman who dated women in her past share the gospel? I even questioned just how this was going to work out! Then, the Lord began to work His strategy and partnered me with a good friend. She'd attended a 'Sunday On Tuesday' service and experienced a life-changing encounter with God. It was all coming together why we had to change the location of our church. We worked strategically together to build this ministry, and God multiplied our efforts.

The Lord often encouraged Reviving Souls through specific words of knowledge and wisdom. For example, one night during our 'Sunday On Tuesday' service, I spoke a word to our congregation, "To Look Again!" It was about things we had done in the past and saw some success, but they seemed to stop working out, so we stopped. None of us at that time understood what things the Lord was speaking of that we should start again. A few of us were entrepreneurs, and we had stopped working our businesses. Little did we know the things we were once involved in were included and speaking truths about sexual perversion.

Over the years, I'd hoped the church would have become more comfortable talking about the Love of God as it relates to the LGBTQ community. There was still the elephant in the room that remained due to a lack of addressing the matter. The Lord was beginning to speak to my heart again about the subject of being born gay. Although I believed it was my story, many others felt the same way and needed someone to explain the narrative. Many in the LBGTQ community believe that their sexuality was not decided by them but after conception. Everyone did not just wake up and make a conscious choice to be gay, knowing the heartache, rejection, and repeatedly being ostracized. We all want to be accepted and loved for who we are. The subject of sexual perversion is vast, and I knew God was calling me to be that voice of reasoning for those of us who wanted a truth that explained why we believed being born gay wasn't a choice.

In 2016, the Lord began speaking about our will and our appetite for things outside His design for human life. Once again, I couldn't dismiss the fact that many gifted people in arts such as dance, singing, playing instruments, prophetic, and natural gifts that serve people who, at some point, have questioned their sexuality. I wish I had statistics, and I know we would all be amazed. Gifted people in the arts, whether in the church or secular, many people already assumed the participants were part of the LBGTQ community. We must ask the question, why do we think that way without sometimes really knowing that information. The reason is we've seen so many gifted people who fit the description above and are part of the LGBTQ community.

When I use the term 'struggle,' I refer to a fight not to practice sin intentionally. We are all tempted to sin or go back to a place of bondage we were delivered. The Bible gives us great scriptures to show us how to resist and how God restores us when needed. *James 4:7 states, "Submit yourselves, therefore, to God. Resist the devil, and he will flee from you." (JUB).* I am so glad that Jesus fulfilled His assignment to die on the cross and shed His Blood to remission sin and those times we fail after salvation. *1 John 1:9 states, " If we confess our sins, he is faithful and just to forgive us our sins and to cleanse us from all unrighteousness" (JUB).*

The Lord began to point out specific correlations through scripture, revealing Lucifer's plan to target some gifts and callings. I understand the enemy hates all of us and wants to keep us from heaven. But he has specifically targeted some of us, and we were born with same-sex attraction. Is it possible to be born with specific flaws? The answer is yes. Abraham's first son from Hagar was born with the character of an untamed donkey who fought against everyone and had a conflict with his relatives. The rejection and abandonment entered his soul from the time of conception, producing a man of war on all levels. Genesis chapter 16 tells this story.

WOW! Lucifer planned a significant revengeful attack on Levites, calling to usher people into God's Presence. Many Levites love God, accept His Son Jesus as their personal Savior, and are committed to serving their churches using their gift. Yet, they live every day with the struggle of pressure to submit to a lifestyle God has not ordained.

Whether we want to admit it or not, some of the most anointed people in our church struggle with same-sex attraction. Some may not have acted upon it, and some have and believe the narrative that they will never have power over the desire.

The word of the Lord clarifies that everything He made was good. ***Genesis 1:31 "And God saw everything that he had made, and, behold, it was very good. And the evening and the morning were the sixth day." (JUB).*** Yet God allowed for the possibility of evil so that we could genuinely serve Him and not out of obligation. He gave Lucifer the same choice to choose Holiness, but he chose evil.

Our God is the creator of the heavens, the earth, the angels, humanity, and animals. Therefore, anytime you are not the creator, it's a given that your creator is superior. So, let's dive into the story of Lucifer's fall from his appointment as God's highest-ranking cherub.

The story of Lucifer is merely fiction for many, and for some scholars, the scriptures are not clear enough to describe the fall of Lucifer. Lucifer became so impressed with his beauty, intelligence, power, and position that he began to desire for himself the honor and glory that belonged to God alone. This pride represents the first sin in the universe—preceding the fall of the human Adam.

In the book of Ezekiel, chapter 28 begins describing a human leader verses 1-10. The verses speak of King Tyre, who God condemned for exalting himself above God, although he was just a man. Many scholars believe that King Tyre and his actions represented Lucifer's mindset and actions. Lucifer was working his anti-God, using King Tyre, the human ruler of the city. The Prophet Ezekiel also gives us glimpses of Lucifer's superhuman creature, who was using, indwelling, in him.

Ezekiel 28 continues to describe a supernatural being beyond a human king. ***Ezekiel 28 12 "You were in Eden, the garden of God; Every precious stone was your covering: The sardius, topaz, and diamond, Beryl, onyx, and jasper, Sapphire, turquoise, and emerald with gold. The workmanship of your timbrels and pipes was prepared for you on the day you were created" (NKJ).*** The scriptures describe a created supernatural creature whose attributes included holiness, beauty, and authority as a leader. But yet iniquity was found in him. The simple definition of iniquity is practiced sin without the intention to change or repent. Lucifer's desire to be worshiped above God caused a breach in his relationship with God. He no longer has access to heaven as a permanent resident. God released him from his duties as a cherub serving the throne of God. ***Ezekiel 28:17 "Your heart was filled with pride because of all your beauty; you corrupted your wisdom for the sake of your splendor. Therefore, I have cast you down to the ground and exposed you helpless before the curious gaze of kings" (TLB). Luke 10:18 "Yes," he told them, "I saw Satan falling from heaven as a flash of lightning" (TLB).***

Job 1:6-7 "One day when the sons of God came to stand in front of the Lord, Satan the Accuser came along with them. 7 The Lord asked Satan, "Where have you come from?"

Satan answered the Lord, "From wandering all over the earth" (GW)? Although Lucifer lost his position and authority in heaven, he visited heaven. The second heaven is his permanent residence until the return of Jesus for the saints.

Many also believe Isaiah 14:12-17 refers to the fall of Lucifer. *Isaiah 14:12-15 "How you are fallen from heaven, O Lucifer, son of the morning! How you are cut down to the ground—mighty though you were against the nations of the world. 13 For you said to yourself, "I will ascend to heaven and rule the angels. I will take the highest throne. I will preside on the Mount of Assembly far away in the north. 14 I will climb to the highest heavens and be like the Most High." 15 But instead, you will be brought down to the pit of hell, down to its lowest depths" (TLB).* These scripture references give us an indication that God had a created being with supernatural abilities, and He deemed no longer an asset to His Kingdom due to pride.

Now you are shaking your head, saying, what does this have to do with LGBTQ. It has everything to do with why I believe some were born with same-sex attractions, including me. As I took a look over my life as an adolescent, I realized same-sex attraction cultivated by Lucifer to ensure my choices later in life would reflect lesbianism. I do not believe God created us to have same-sex attraction. Because the desires seem natural and have been with many since childhood, it seems the only logical reason is God made these emotions and desires.

Many believe the Bible does not address the subject of homosexuality as a sin. The scripture *1 Corinthians 6:9-11 9 "Know ye not that the unrighteous shall not*

230

inherit the kingdom of God? Be not deceived: neither fornicators, nor idolaters, nor adulterers, nor effeminate, nor abusers of themselves with mankind, 10 Nor thieves, nor covetous, nor drunkards, nor revilers, nor extortioners, shall inherit the kingdom of God. 11 And such were some of you: but ye are washed, but ye are sanctified, but ye are justified in the name of the Lord Jesus, and by the Spirit of our God" (KJV). The word effeminate is the translated Greek word '***Malakos***,' which means a male submits his body to unnatural lewdness, indicating homosexuality. Apostle Paul listed these sins that are against the principles of God, and repentance is needed to inherit the Kingdom of God. There was a time in my life when I no longer desired change and practiced lesbianism without conviction. I became reprobate and didn't care if I died in my iniquity. But thank God for the prayers of the righteous. The prayers kept the enemy of my soul from taking my life during that rebellious season. So, God does not discriminate against the different types of sin, and He is ready to forgive and wash all with His Blood shed on Calvary's Cross. The church must stop condemning the LGBTQ community and suggesting no hope is available.

Let's talk a little further about why it is possible to be born with same-sex attraction. The Bible says God created Adam and Eve in the likeness of His image, and they were perfect. God gave Adam and Eve one command; do not eat from the tree of knowledge. But Eve listened to the serpent, also known as Lucifer, and believed his story that they were lower than God, and He was protecting His image. Once Adam ate from the tree of knowledge, they became subject to the plans of Lucifer to create havoc in their spiritual and natural lives. We see the first example of jealousy and

231

murder between brothers. Now sin has formed and is now being passed down through generations.

In our soulish realms are our dislikes and appetites. If we are honest, we can name specific patterns within our family, whether good or bad. In some cases, we have become accustomed to these patterns and praise them even when detrimental. Change for the better can be challenging, but God has provided a way of escape from cycles designed to harm us and keep growth stagnating. Intercession can root out the plan of Lucifer in the lives of our families.

When we read the story of King David, he acknowledges his sin by stating, ***"But I was born a sinner, yes, from the moment my mother conceived me. Psalm 51:5 (TLB).*** King David's confession of his sin reveals that iniquity was present at the time of conception, and the ability to sin came with him as he entered this world. We have proof through the scriptures that we all come here with appetites against the things of God. Have you ever asked a toddler if they did something wrong, and they shake their head no, but you know better? No one taught them how to lie, but they are already trying to cover up the crime. LOL!

I have watched people gifted in the arts, hospitality, and creative servers over the years. Whether they are in church or not, many are part of the LGBTQ community or choose to live a single life practicing sexual abstinence. Many people look at these gifts and automatically assume their lifestyle identifies as gay. Come on, let's be honest; we think all-male choir directors, male hairstylists, and male make-up artists are gay. Some also think women pastors/preachers, female barbers, female musicians, or females in male-dominated positions are gay. So, why is this part of most people's thinking? Because many are no longer hiding their sexuality. They have accepted what they feel and refuse to live in secret.

Then there is the church. Some ministries preach against homosexuality but do not preach against the other sins with the same vigor. The gifts in the church who are not part of a gay-affirming church act out the policy "Don't Ask, Don't Tell!" While preaching, some churches describe it as unconquerable unpardonable and add Adam and Steve and Eve and Evelyn as jokes to prove their point. Let me just set the record straight. God's plan of salvation and redemption is more powerful than any sin we can ever commit. God sent His Son, Jesus, to shed His Blood to remission sins. Condemning certain sins to hell attempting to discriminate against God's Mercy and Grace is not a believer's character. Despite the discrepancies related to homosexuality, many still attend church because they love God. The same-sex attraction struggles appear never to end, and some have just given up trying to abstain from engaging in the homosexual lifestyle. I understand this because I, too, gave up, stopped attending church, and practiced the lesbian lifestyle with no intent to sacrifice my desires.

Romans 11:29 "God never changes his mind when he gives gifts or when he calls someone" (GW). Well, I couldn't get to the next point without talking about the gifts given to man by God. Lucifer was beautiful and given gifts by God. He is a created being. In other words, he did not make himself, nor did he give himself gifts. Let's refer back to the scripture in *Ezekiel 28:13 "You were in Eden, the garden of God; Every precious stone was your covering: The sardius, topaz, and diamond, Beryl, onyx, and jasper, Sapphire, turquoise, and emerald with gold. The workmanship of your timbrels and pipe Was prepared for you on the day you were created" (NKJV).* Lucifer's creativity gave him the title of the morning star. He was one of the chief angels whose wings covered God's throne in heaven, and he led all the other angels around the throne as they worshiped God. As he glorified God, the light from his body permeated the heavens. An angelic sound of harps, voices, and percussion not known to man by Lucifer crowned him as the leader of worship. There was no other angel like him and given the ultimate job of bringing glory to the Most High God. But because of his extraordinary abilities and beauty, he exalted himself above God and all other created beings like him.

Lucifer's punishment for his rebellion caused him to seek revenge against humankind. I know you are scratching your head but hold on. Remember, gifts are given to men whether we accept the plan of salvation or not. God ordains our call or gifting before conception. In other words, He speaks, and all heaven becomes aware of our gifts. So, therefore people can use their talents in church and never be convicted to live their best life for the Lord. They view using their gifts as a job only. They become spiritual employees who clock in and out of the church and live without conviction. God will not remove one's gift due to not accepting salvation. Because of that, many feel there is no change needed. Lucifer is also banking on that thought process to deceive as many as he can.

I must tell you that those of us who have gifts like Lucifer have a target on our back! He is angry, and he recognizes his replacements. My God!!! He can't stand that we lead others into worship through music or the preached word, and we flow in our creativity while serving others. Transforming others to be beautiful and handsome reminds him of his beauty. He aims to make our lives miserable and chaotic, emotionally challenging. The truth is that many of us have fought so hard to be happy, but it rarely shows up because of the fight in our souls. He understands that he can't take our job away as his replacement, so Lucifer uses the only weapon he has. Our souls have become his weapon. Once he recognizes those called out to replace him, he enters our soul once conceived. Then he unravels a plan to cultivate the seed in our souls. Lucifer uses molestation, abandonment, and rejection as significant players to grow the root of sexual perversion, specifically homosexuality. Why does homosexuality seem to be his object of revenge?

Lucifer longs for creatures to worship him. The one-third of the angels that went with him is not enough. He wants to defile God's plan of giving men his gifts and job. The definition of homosexuality for most is about the act of same-sex attraction engaging in the lifestyle. Lucifer views it as one worshiping their body over God's plan for relationships for humankind. His fall from heaven came from his worship of himself. So, homosexuality is the worship of our body over God's plan. Spiritually, Lucifer wants others to worship themselves by engaging in homosexuality, glorifying him. His other plan is to stop us from procreation. God uses procreation to duplicate gifts on the earth. Families of Levites, Priests, Dancers, Cooks, workers in the church. Looking at your family, I'm sure you can see the same gifts duplicated down through generations.

Over the years, I've realized so many have felt hopelessly trapped because the desire feels natural for same-sex attraction. I'm not here to tell you God is holding it against you because of your desires. But what He requires is that we press to sacrifice our wants when they are not part of

235

His plan for our lives. Jesus experienced a crucial time in His life and didn't want to yield self-sacrifice for His call. The Garden of Gethsemane, *Luke 22:42-44 "42 "He walked away, perhaps a stone's throw, and knelt down and prayed this prayer: "Father, if you are willing, please take away this cup of horror from me. But I want your will, not mine." 43 Then an angel from heaven appeared and strengthened him, 44 for he was in such agony of spirit that he broke into a sweat of blood, with great drops falling to the ground as he prayed more and more earnestly" (TLB).* Reading the story of the anguish, sweat, and compromise needed to please the Father encourages my heart. You see, God is looking for our sacrifice, and He accepts our brokenness. Lucifer is happy when we use our talent for God and not sacrifice our lifestyle. Our gifts don't Glorify God; they are used to help others. Our sacrifice to live a life pleasing to God is what brings honor and glory to our God.

Many of our Gospel artists struggle, and I know they love God, but they can't seem to understand why they have same-sex attraction. I saw in a vision a very prominent Gospel Artist who was terminally ill, asking God for forgiveness. The Lord revealed to me that many of them have died a slow death so they would have time to repent for the iniquity that seemed to be a way of life. He said those who followed the artist; if they knew he admitted his wrong, they would also strive not to practice their iniquity. My heart aches when I see leaders and other gifted people working their gifts, believing their anointing to perform the talent excludes them from judgment. *Matthew 7:22-23 "22 Many will say to me in that day, Lord, Lord, have we not prophesied in thy name? and in thy name have cast out devils? And in thy name done many wonderful works? 23 And then will I profess unto them, I never knew you: depart from me, ye that work iniquity" (KJV).*

I have also had friends I prayed for healing from various sicknesses, including AIDS, and God said I was taking their lives in the earth realm and would not allow Lucifer to mock them anymore. He gave them space to confess their faults. Another friend of mine appeared in a night vision and said he was tired, and God took him a few days later. A few days after his death, in another night vision, the Lord brought him to encourage me to keep sharing truths. While sitting under your teaching, he expressed the strength and knowledge to overcome and live a life of victory more than any other time in his Christian walk. He said you have no idea how many people in the church are struggling. The Holy Spirit overshadowed me when I awakened, and tears began to fall. The love, mercy, and grace God extend to His people is beyond our comprehension. And He will not allow Lucifer to win and take more souls into eternal damnation.

The Father created all things to worship Him. Humankind and angels have a choice to accept Him and worship Him without compromise. They could also operate in their gifts and talents and not serve God. Lucifer chose a third of the angels to do the impossible overthrow of His creator. On the other hand, we have the opportunity to replace Lucifer as a worshiper unto God. What makes humankind so unique is we accept the plan of redemption by repentance, and we practice submitting our desires, wants, and appetites to the Lord. Lucifer's pride revolted against refraining from his opinion of being more significant than

237

God, and he began to lust after a position designed for the Creator. As we study the Bible, we see examples of men failing because they went after things, seats of authority, and accomplishments. Some lost their kingdoms, lives, and their right standing with God.

Many disagree that homosexuality is a sin, and I understand the thought process. I'm not sharing these truths to harm or to condemn. But I want you to know God chose you to serve His people. It is not a coincidence that many of us anointed in certain areas feel like we were born homosexual. Lucifer's plans included placing the appetite into our souls, which were foul and have caused much grief in our lives. Ostracized and loved at the same time because of our anointing. What should we do? Should we leave God, leave the church, and give in to the label given by Lucifer. The answer is no, and because we now understand the battle, it's worth sacrificing not to engage in the same-sex attraction we experience. I know it's unfair, but we deal with a ruthless angel who wants us not to occupy his space in heaven. God's mercy and grace are at our reach when we need it most. The Lord instructed me to pray for a gospel artist I saw in a night vision. The gospel artist was very sick and laid on his couch with a high fever while talking with me. *"He said God had blessed me tremendously in my career. I have number one songs on the billboard and performed for many. But if I could change some of the decisions made. I would have served God with my body also. He said to tell them not to do what I've done engaging in homosexuality."* Since that vision, I've continued to pray for the psalmist, musicians, creativity creators, dancers, female leaders, or simply the Levites and others who filled positions described earlier.

Maybe you are reading this book, and you've given up. Let me encourage you that it's not too late. Take this time to begin to talk to the Lord. Accept His Son Jesus into your heart. Well, I know you are saying I'm part of the LGBTQ community, and that's where I belong. I'm not asking you to dismiss your same-sex attraction; I'm asking you to form a relationship with Jesus. In Him, I found love, no condemnation, and strength when needed. Yes, I know some have treated you as an outcast, but let me say I'm sorry for the unjust ridicule you've faced because of who God called you to be. God is not concerned about your sexual orientation, but your sacrifice to worship Him in spirit and truth, including your body, brings Glory to God. The scripture gives us hope; *Romans 3:23 -24 "23 " Yes, all have sinned; all fall short of God's glorious ideal; 24 yet now God declares us "not guilty" of offending him if we trust in Jesus Christ, who in his kindness freely takes away our sins" (TLB).*

I have great compassion for all of us who have lived with this war in our souls since we can remember. Our appearance, mannerisms, thoughts, desires are misunderstood as to who's the fault for the way we appear. Yet, our gifts made room in the lives of our family, friends, and those we served. A tug of war is the only thing that comes to mind to describe this life at times. The thoughts battling which way we should follow and be at peace. Trust me; if you took a survey, no one would have chosen to contend with all the complications that come with the call of a worshiper. But the truth is we pay the price to lead others into the presence of God, flexing our creativity in places needed and bringing beauty to the eye of the beholder.

The call upon me includes intercession for my brothers and sisters, who Lucifer has targeted. I watch them move forward regardless of the mental anguish and need for acceptance. Many nights tears roll down my face as I cry out to God to strengthen the Levite who's having thoughts of suicide. Oh yes, those thoughts often crossed my mind. We asked God to take away the appetite to worship our body over Him. But we're reminded that we have a promise through a dialogue Apostle Paul gives the church. *I Corinthians 12:8-10 "8 For this thing I besought the Lord three times that it might be taken from me. 9 And he said unto me, My grace is sufficient for thee; for my strength is made perfect in weakness. Most gladly, therefore, I will rather glory in my weaknesses that the power of Christ may dwell in me. 10 Therefore I am content in weaknesses, in reproaches, in necessities, in persecutions, in distresses for Christ's sake, for when I am weak, then am I strong " (JUB).*

I gave up believing something was wrong with me and that I woke one morning and decided to be a lesbian; instead, I chose to believe who God says I am, 'Lucifer's Replacement!' There is no way we can dismiss who God says we are, and it does not matter how far we try to run from God, and it's impossible to separate from the call which all heaven bears witness to God's assignments.

Pray this prayer with me. Father, I come giving you all my fears and flaws. I admit to all my wrongs. And I believe you died and shed your blood for my sins. Forgive me and provide a clean heart. I renounce the label Lucifer placed on my life. I accept the plan you have for my life. Please fill me with your Holy Spirit leading me and always comforting me.

Thank you for your Mercy and Grace! By praying that prayer, you have received Jesus in your life or received restoration. I admonish you to find a gathering that teaches the word of God meticulously with love and patience. I encourage you that you have an advocate with the Father, and He'll never leave you.

Psalm 46:1 " God is our refuge and strength, a tested help in times of trouble" (TLB8). Don't be consumed with your same-sex attraction but be an overcomer with love for God who pledges to give you strength to worship Him. Most people do not wish to believe that Jesus experienced same-sex attraction temptation. No, I have not lost my mind; let's look at the word of God. *Hebrew 4:15 "15 We have a chief priest who is able to sympathize with our weaknesses. He was tempted in every way that we are, but he didn't sin" (GWT).* There you have it, and yes, temptation found Jesus, but His conditioning in the presence of God through worship empowered His ability to resist sin and please His Father in all areas. Scriptures are pillars we can lean on when our faith becomes weak. Never give up working out your soul's salvation. Our failures aren't too much for Jesus. The love of God surrounds us and never weakens towards us. For that, I am thankful, and I will never give up on working the call upon my life and living a life of sacrifice. I am Lucifer's replacement, and you are Lucifer's replacement. God has settled on His choice, and it is us, humankind. The Love of God will prevail, and Lucifer will meet his fate for his attack against his replacements.

www.ingramcontent.com/pod-product-compliance
Lightning Source LLC
Chambersburg PA
CBHW020444130626
46549CB00001B/296